A SUPERNATURAL PRAYER LIFE

D1603803

Nancy Dufresne

TABLE OF CONTENTS

INTRODUCTION v

CHAPTER ONE 7
Heard in Heaven

CHAPTER TWO 15
A Supernatural Prayer Life

CHAPTER THREE 25
Privileges of Being Filled With the Spirit

CHAPTER FOUR 43
Living Full of the Spirit

CHAPTER FIVE 53
Quieting the Mind

CHAPTER SIX 59
Edifying Yourself

CHAPTER SEVEN 67
Edifying Defined

CHAPTER EIGHT 101
Other Benefits of Speaking in Tongues

CHAPTER NINE 107
"Let Him Pray"

CHAPTER TEN 111
Making Power Available

CHAPTER ELEVEN 123
Continuing in Prayer

CHAPTER TWELVE 127
    The Spirit of Prayer
RECOMMENDED READING ON PRAYER 149

INTRODUCTION

The spirit of prayer is as diversified as the Spirit Himself. There are patterns that the Spirit may lead one in, but how broad is His range. There's always more to know and farther to go when following the Holy Spirit in conducting Kingdom business.

Much has been written on the subject of prayer, and I don't seek to duplicate those teachings, but I am stirred to put what I have learned during times of prayer into book form so that others may be instructed and encouraged in this divine direction of prayer.

The subject of prayer, being so vast, cannot be completely taught in one book, so I intend to only focus on aspects of prayer which I am prompted by the Spirit of God to address.

Every believer has a royal invitation from God Himself to "*come boldly unto the throne of grace, that we may obtain mercy, and find grace to help in time of need*" (Hebrews 4:16). The Amplified Bible of this verse reads:

> *Let us then fearlessly and confidently and boldly draw near to the throne of grace...that we may receive mercy [for our failures] and find grace to help in good time for every need [appropriate help and well-timed help, coming just when we need it].*

The throne is the place of obtaining. No need goes unmet at the throne. No question goes unanswered at the throne.

We are children of the throne. We belong there.

What a privilege has been given to us as God's children to have such an invitation to conduct Kingdom business with His throne! There is no expiration date to this invitation at His throne; you can come as often as you like, and stay as long as you will. How many times we have forfeited our place in His presence by being occupied with the unimportant and unfruitful? May we all learn that the business of God's kingdom is to hold its proper place in our life, and without giving proper attention to this great privilege of prayer, we forfeit much – not only for our own lives, but for the lives of others who need the influence of the throne.

CHAPTER ONE

Heard in Heaven

I don't believe in prayer; I believe in the God who hears and answers prayer! I don't magnify the act of praying; I magnify the God who hears and answers when I pray!

Prayer does not change things; the God who hears and answers prayer is the One who changes things when believing prayer is made. Prayer does play a role in change by inviting God to move, but God is the One who changes things.

Jesus stood before Lazarus' tomb, lifted up His eyes and said, *"Father, I thank thee that thou hast HEARD me. And I knew that thou HEAREST me always..."* (John 11:41 & 42).

Jesus didn't say, "Father, I thank You that I am the Messiah." He didn't say, "I thank You that I am anointed." He didn't say, "I thank You that miracles are performed at My hands." Although all those things are true about Jesus, Jesus wasn't thanking His Father for those things when He stood in front of Lazarus' grave.

When Jesus was faced with death, the thing He confessed, and the thing He reminded Himself of, was that He was heard by God.

When you're faced with need, remind yourself, and confess that God hears you when you pray; He hears you when you talk to Him.

What did He thank the Father for when He was faced with a great need? He thanked His Father that He heard Him! To know that God hears you holds you calm, even when faced with great obstacles and tests. To be heard in Heaven is to be assured of the answer!

Notice what the Spirit said through John in 1 John 5:14 & 15:

And this is the confidence that we have in him, that, if we ask any thing according to his will, HE HEARETH US: And if we KNOW that he HEARS us, whatsoever we ask, we know that we HAVE the petitions that we desired of him.

According to this passage, we see that to be *heard* by God is to have – to have the petitions that we desire of Him. Being heard equals the having.

Jesus knew this as He prayed while standing before Lazarus' tomb. He knew that to be *heard* by God was to *have* the request granted. That's why Jesus thanked the Father for hearing Him; He knew the request was granted.

I'm so thankful I have a Father who hears! I'm so thankful I have a Father who is listening for me!

If we really believed that we are heard in heaven, if we really believed that God answers us when He hears us, we would make more requests.

It's not the act of praying that grants your requests – it's a hearing Father! Therefore, we don't magnify the act of

8

praying; rather, we magnify our wonderful Father who hears.

There are millions in this world who pray daily to Buddha, to a Hindu god, or to some other false god, but there comes no help to them because their god doesn't hear them. Therefore, their act of praying means nothing. No praying does any good except that prayer be heard. Apart from a hearing God, prayer is fruitless; it accomplishes nothing.

The God of Heaven is the only One who hears! He is listening for the prayers of His people. He answers all He hears that is prayed in line with His Word.

There are Buddhist monks who reside in their Buddhist temples, devoting themselves to a life of prayer. But their zeal and persistence in prayer will bring no answer when praying to a god who has no ears. If it was the *act* of praying that brought help, these Buddhist monks would receive their help; but they don't receive help from the one they pray to, because it's not the act of praying that brings help. Help comes when the prayer is heard and answered, and our Heavenly Father is the only hearing God.

If a Christian magnifies the *act* of praying, they will become prideful because they pray. If a Christian magnifies the *act* of praying, they will become works-minded regarding prayer; they will tie their faith to how much they pray, and begin measuring their success as a believer by how much they pray. But we don't pray to earn anything from God. We pray because we know we have a Father who hears, and since we know He hears us, we also know we have the answer to our prayer; we know our Word-based prayers are granted because He hears us (1 John 5:14 & 15).

9

We don't study our Bible or pray to earn anything from God, or to qualify to receive something from Him. We study our Bible and pray so that we may know Him better, and know all that He has provided for us. The understanding of this keeps us free from getting trapped into a lifestyle of works of the law, which kills the life of fellowship with Him.

A fellowship and private devotional time with God that's based on works, measuring how much time we study or pray, is a devotional time that will have no life flowing in it; it will be dry and full of duty, and produce no fruit, and will only bring bondage into the life of the one praying.

We don't magnify the act of praying, we magnify the God who hears. We are so convinced of His willingness to hear and to answer His children; we are so convinced of His great love for us, that we look for opportunities to spend time with Him. We would not want to diminish the privilege of being heard by God by bringing this high honor down to measuring it by the clock, or by becoming proud of ourselves for the time spent praying.

Rather, we live ever mindful of Him, and we keep our hearts turned toward Him all day, living a life that prays, living in unbroken fellowship with the One who hears. We are to allow conversation with Him to flow as freely as it would with our nearest and dearest friend. He is more than any dear friend; He is that One who abides within through the Person of the Holy Spirit, and He is worthy of our full attention and adoration.

Anytime we are talking to God, we are praying. Let's be genuine in speaking to Him; let's speak freely from our hearts, and shun all formality and coldness when we engage ourselves in fellowship with Him, the One who hears.

Prayer doesn't change things – God changes things! As we ask in faith and believe that He hears us, we are His co-laborers. We pray in faith, but He's the One who makes changes as men respond to Him. If our prayers changed things, then we could take the credit, but it's God who changes things as men cooperate with Him; therefore, He receives all the credit and all the glory.

To every victory, there is man's side and there is God's side. As man fulfills his part, then God fulfills His part; but we are never to magnify man's side, we magnify God's side. To magnify man's part is to take credit and glory; but to magnify God's side is to give Him credit and glory. Without God's side, man's side is useless, so all honor and glory goes to Him.

GOD HEARS US ALWAYS

When Jesus stood before Lazarus' tomb that day, He not only thanked His Father for hearing Him, but He also declared, *"And I knew that thou hearest me ALWAYS..."* Jesus knew that His Father didn't just hear Him when He directed a prayer to Him, but Jesus knew that God was hearing Him always! Even when Jesus was talking to men, God was hearing Him. The way you speak among men will affect your speaking to God.

Four days prior to the day Jesus stood in front of Lazarus' grave, He received word that Lazarus was sick and near death. But Jesus replied to the messengers (He wasn't directing a prayer to God): *"This sickness is not unto death, but for the glory of God, that the Son of God might be glorified thereby"* (John 11:4).

Jesus knew the final outcome of Lazarus' situation would not be death, but that God would receive glory by Lazarus being raised up.

It mattered what Jesus said to those men when He first heard the report of Lazarus' sickness – God was hearing Him! So, when Jesus stood before Lazarus' tomb, what He spoke there was in line with what He spoke to the messengers four days earlier.

You can't talk one way with people, then talk another way when praying to God, and expect to get results. You can't talk words of doubt and unbelief about a situation to someone, and then be able to exercise full faith when speaking to God. God hears you when you pray, but He hears you always; He hears if words of doubt are spoken to others.

James tells us that a double-minded man is unstable in all his ways, and to not let that man think that he will receive anything of the Lord (James 1:7 & 8). Jesus was single-minded about Lazarus' sickness. He spoke the same things to the messengers who brought word of Lazarus' sickness as He did when He stood before Lazarus' grave. His words agreed in both locations, when speaking to men and to God.

But the man who speaks double-minded, one way to people but another way to God, won't receive from the Lord because he forgot that God hears him always – not just when he prays, but when he's among men.

KNOWLEDGE DOESN'T EQUAL PERMISSION

John Wesley, who was the founder of the Methodist revival, stated, "God is limited by our prayer life. It seems that He can do nothing for humanity unless someone asks Him."

Is this a correct observation by John Wesley? Absolutely, it is! Let's find out why.

Matthew 6:8 records that Jesus stated, *"For your Father KNOWETH what things ye have need of, before ye ask him."* Toward the end of His earthly ministry, Jesus instructed His disciples,

> *Hitherto (up to this time) have ye asked nothing in my name: ASK, and ye shall receive, that your joy may be full.*
>
> (John 16:24)

Notice what these two scriptures say. The first one tells us that God knows what we have need of even before we ask, and the second one invites us to ask so that we'll receive.

Someone may wonder, "Well, if God knows what we have need of even before we ask, why do we even have to ask? Why doesn't God give it to us if He knows we need it?"

The answer is this – knowledge doesn't equal permission. Just because God knows that someone has need of something doesn't mean that He has their permission to move in their behalf and give them what they need.

If a friend came to visit me, and parked his car in my driveway, just because I have knowledge that his car is in

13

my driveway doesn't give me permission to get in it and drive it.

If a person sitting next to me in a church service pulls out his wallet and I happen to see several hundred dollar bills in his wallet, just because I know they have that money doesn't give me permission to take it. Knowledge doesn't equal permission.

Likewise, the knowledge God has about all of our lives doesn't give Him permission to move in our behalf.

God doesn't violate anyone's will and move for them without their permission. God can't move in someone's life uninvited.

That's even true regarding salvation. God knew the world needed a Savior, so He sent Jesus. But that Savior doesn't come into their hearts just because God knows they need Him – they still must ask; they must ask Jesus to come into their hearts.

God doesn't force anything on anyone; that's how the devil and evil spirits work, but not God.

God only moves where He's invited to move.

Even though God knows what someone may need, they must still ask God before they will receive what they need. Yet, the Word assures us that when we ask, we shall receive, for God hears us when we pray!

CHAPTER TWO

A Supernatural Prayer Life

The heart of every man, saved or unsaved, is hungry for the supernatural. God created man in His own image, and God is supernatural; therefore, man longs for the supernatural. No man is fulfilled or satisfied living a natural, carnal life. His insides reach out for more than what this natural realm possesses. Man longs to see what this realm doesn't show.

But, as those who are born again, we have a free invitation to live in the realm that every man longs for – the supernatural realm. The Word calls it the "unseen" realm, the spirit realm; it is the realm of the supernatural.

Jesus came from the unseen realm and showed man that there was another realm, a higher realm, than this seen realm that's visible to all. Jesus walked in this seen realm among men, but He manifested the unseen realm that hungry men long for.

The unseen realm is the realm our Father lives in. It's the realm that is greater than this realm. It's the realm that dominates and governs this realm. It's the realm of the highest authority. We are children of the unseen realm.

God instructs us to:

...look not at the things which are seen, but at the things which are not seen: for the things which are

seen are temporal; but the things which are not seen are eternal.

(Second Corinthians 4:18)

To live according to this seen realm, and to focus only on the realm we see, is to live disappointed and dissatisfied. This seen realm doesn't author the things that satisfy the heart of a hungry man. To live with our eyes riveted to this realm is to be cheated of what it means to really live. Every life will manifest the realm they are occupied with; they will manifest the realm they are focused on.

Those of us who are born again are children of the unseen realm; we are children of God's realm, children of the throne, children of God's kingdom, and His kingdom is not of this world. The unseen realm is the realm of our Father.

Jesus showed us what God's realm, the supernatural, unseen realm, has for this seen world. By the power of God, Jesus worked miracles, healings, and great demonstrations of power that weren't authored with this natural realm; they were manifestations of the unseen realm – God's realm.

Sickness, disease, heartbreak, lack and defeat are a part of this world. Jesus was an intrusion into this seen realm; with His entrance, He manifested God's realm of healing, health, supply, peace, victory, and all else that belongs to the realm of God.

All difficulties and failures are of the seen realm, but all answers, successes and victories are of God's realm.

This natural realm is the realm of impossibilities, but God's realm is the realm of all possibilities. There are limits to the natural realm, but there are no limits in the unseen realm.

EVERY MAN MUST CHOOSE HIS WORLD

Jesus not only revealed God's realm to man, showing its utter dominion over all the things in this natural realm, but He made a declaration that invited change to every man's world when He declared, *"I am the door...no man cometh unto the Father, but by me"* (John 10:9 & 14:6). He was letting us know, that as the Door, He is the Door between the two worlds. Now there is to be free exchange between the two realms. Those of us in the seen realm can freely access all the benefits of the unseen realm, and the unseen realm can find entrance to the seen realm.

The Door between the two worlds is now open. Every man must choose his world!

Which world will you live in? Which one will dominate you? The choice is yours.

We have the grand invitation God offered to all His children: *"Come boldly unto the throne of grace, that we may obtain..."* (Hebrews 4:16). The invitation is sent. You can come as often as you like, and stay as long as you will. There are no time limits or restraints. Jesus is the open Door to the Father's throne. We are children of the Throne. We belong to the Throne.

Under the Old Covenant, the people of God didn't have free access to the presence of God because Jesus had not yet made the way open to the presence of God. But God's desire to bless them was so great, that through the prophet

Malachi, God told His people that He would pour out blessings upon them through the windows of heaven. But since Jesus came, we aren't limited to operating through heaven's windows. Jesus, the open Door, has swung wide free access to the Father's throne, and has made us children of the Throne. Now we can come boldly to the throne and obtain all we need.

Nothing goes unanswered at the throne. Nothing has ever stumped or mystified the throne – it is the place of "obtaining."

A TEACHER FROM THE UNSEEN REALM

Since the spirit realm is unseen to the natural eye, we won't know about that realm until we're taught about it. The Word of God is the only book that reveals to us the spirit realm that we cannot see with our physical eyes.

Not only do we have God's Word to reveal to us the spirit realm, but God sent us a Person who is of the unseen realm to be our Guide and Teacher about that realm – the Holy Spirit.

God sent Jesus, Who is the open Door to the unseen realm, so that we could live in that realm; but then He sent the Person of the Holy Spirit to be our tutor concerning the unseen realm.

The Holy Spirit has not come to just teach us how to have success in this seen, natural realm, but He's come to help us learn of and live in the unseen realm, the realm of the supernatural. As we follow Him, our Guide, and become proficient in operating in that unseen realm, we are able to manifest the blessings and power of the unseen realm into this natural realm; then we'll live days of heaven on this earth.

When Jesus was baptized in the Jordan River by John the Baptist, the Holy Spirit descended upon Jesus in the form of a dove; from that day on, Jesus manifested the unseen realm among men. Healings, miracles, signs and wonders were worked – all manifestations of the unseen realm, the supernatural realm.

On the Day of Pentecost, as the 120 disciples gathered in an upper room in Jerusalem expecting the arrival of the Holy Spirit, His entrance broke into this realm as a mighty wind. The sound was heard by all; then His presence became visible to all as tongues of fire sat upon each of their heads. This divine Tutor, Teacher, Guide of the unseen realm had arrived.

All who would receive this mighty Spirit, this Person of the unseen realm, could now operate upon this earth as Jesus did. Through them is to manifest the great power of the unseen realm that flows from God; manifesting healings, miracles, signs and wonders, which are the will of the Father. Those who know the Holy Spirit best, those who follow Him the closest, will manifest the unseen realm more fully and accurately.

The Holy Spirit is now present upon the earth, dwelling in men who will receive Him, and making the Father's will visible through those who will cooperate with Him.

BE FILLED WITH THE HOLY GHOST

Every man who receives Jesus is born of the Spirit; he has the *indwelling* of the Spirit. However, there is another experience that we see in the Word that is available to all of God's children, which is the infilling of the Holy Spirit. This *infilling* of the Holy Spirit is evidenced by speaking in other tongues (Acts 2).

Jesus told His disciples that once the Holy Spirit filled them, they would walk in a power that they had never known before (Acts 1:8). It was the same Person of power that came upon Him at His baptism, and outfitted Him with the power and ability to fulfill His purpose on the earth. Jesus dared not send His disciples out to accomplish Kingdom business without this infilling of power.

No man can fully accomplish all God has called him to without being filled with the Holy Spirit.

How does one receive the infilling of the Holy Spirit? The same way anything is received from God – through faith. Tell the Father that you see in the Word that the Holy Spirit is a free gift to His children (Acts 2:38). Ask Him to fill you with the Holy Spirit, and then believe He does fill you and thank Him for it. Then start speaking out the words and utterances that flow up from your spirit; start speaking out in other tongues. The words don't come from your mind, but they come up from down in your spirit. Speak those words out. God won't move your mouth for you, but as you begin to speak, the utterances will flow up from your spirit.

This infilling of the Holy Spirit is a divine gift that belongs to every one of God's children who will receive Him. He belongs to you to help you fulfill the greatness of God's plan for your life.

THE MAN WHO WALKS WITH GOD

The man who knows how to hold fast to God's Word in the face of all opposition, and knows the Spirit of God, working in full cooperation with Him, is the man who brings the greatest blessings to this earth.

There have been many men of genius in the scientific, medical, engineering, and financial worlds, but no man makes an impact on humanity like a man of the Word and the Spirit – a man made brilliant by the Holy Ghost. The man who makes a supernatural, lasting difference in the earth is a man who walks with God in His own realm, a man who keeps pace with God, a man who lives full of the Spirit, wholly yielded to the Spirit, a man who knows the moving of the Spirit, a man who is acquainted with and proficient in cooperating with the Spirit, a man whose life is fragranced with God's presence. No idle dreamer takes hold of this kind of a life; but the one who takes time to live full of the Word of God, the one who knows the Spirit of God, walks in a place that few men find.

WHAT DO YOU GIVE YOURSELF TO?

Men will spend countless hours, travel great distances, and spend small fortunes to be in the presence of a man who has developed his mind, talents and skills, and has risen to the top in his field. Yet, we too often fall short when it comes to taking time to sit under the tutorship of the Holy Spirit. We'll do much to develop our minds and skills, yet leave the development of our own spirits woefully neglected.

Acts 6 records that in the face of increase, the disciples had to make a definite decision to continue to give themselves to prayer and the ministry of the Word. God gave them increase, but He didn't give it to them so they would neglect their spiritual privileges of prayer and the ministry of the Word.

Don't allow increase to pull you away from your spiritual priorities. Increase is no good reason to neglect your own spiritual progress.

It may be an increase of people, as in Acts 6, or an increase in business, or an increase in position and responsibility, but in the face of all increase, the man's spiritual life must take precedence.

It is to be understood that it was the preachers, those in the full-time ministry, who committed to continue to give themselves to prayer and the ministry of the Word, while successful, spiritual businessmen were assigned the responsibilities of carrying out the business side of the ministry. But even still, these businessmen were to be full of the Spirit. They conducted their daily business responsibilities, but they also made their own spiritual advancement a priority.

No matter what your station in life, take time to be a student of the Word and a student of the Holy Spirit. The

Word of God is a *divine* Word; it needs a divine Teacher. The unseen realm of God is a supernatural realm; it requires a supernatural Teacher. We have that Teacher in the Person of the Holy Spirit. We must become acquainted with the Holy Spirit, be sensitive to His movements, and cooperate with His guidance.

There is another realm. There is a higher realm we must learn and respond to.

The realm of God is the realm of things to come. There are no unknowns in the realm of God. There are no questions in the realm of God – only answers. Questions are the children of a lack of knowledge. There is no lack of knowledge, understanding, or wisdom in God's realm. Answers are of the realm of God – the realm of revelation. We are children of that realm.

CHAPTER THREE

Privileges of Being Filled With the Spirit

As children of a supernatural Father, we are to live supernatural lives – lives that are manifesting the blessings of the unseen realm. The Word of God reveals that supernatural, unseen world, and the Holy Spirit reveals the Word to us.

To live in the supernatural realm that the Word makes known to us, we must learn to fully cooperate with the Word and the Spirit. To hear and respond to the Spirit of God, you must develop your own human spirit.

You are a spirit, you have a soul (which is made up of your mind, your will and your emotions), and you live in a body.

When God speaks to you, and when He guides you, He's going to do it through your spirit. He won't lead you through your mind, or your body, but He leads you through your spirit.

Therefore, to know His voice and His leadings, your spirit must be developed. The believer develops his spirit through feeding and acting on the Word of God.

But another primary way to develop your spirit and make your spirit sensitive to the Holy Spirit, is by speaking much in other tongues. If your spirit is dull and insensitive to the Spirit's leadings, it will cost you much in life, and you will imprison your own spirit and sentence yourself to live a life in the natural, unable to distinguish and recognize the great movings of God.

We are not called to live natural lives, but supernatural lives.

NEVER MISS IT AGAIN

We are made in God's image; therefore, we are to share in His success. Since the greater One is on the inside of every believer, and He has never failed, it is possible for us to never fail or never miss it again if we will wholly follow Him. He never leads us into failure. If we fail, it is our own doings and not His; we were following our own ways, and not His guidance.

If we would develop our spirits, making ourselves sensitive to the leadings of the Spirit, we would never go another wrong direction in life; we would never make another wrong business move; we would never make another bad financial investment; we would never marry the wrong person; we would never be found among wrong fellowship; we would never make mistakes with our children; we would never buy the wrong house, take the wrong job, hire the wrong employees, or make any other missed step.

Many of life's trials, tragedies and heartaches are due to having spirits that are not sensitive to the Holy Spirit. He will lead us into total success if we will hear Him and follow.

26

A SUCCESSFUL PRAYER LIFE

He will also lead us into total success in our prayer lives if we will be sensitive to the Spirit, hear the Spirit and follow the Spirit.

The prayer lives of many Christians are dry, ineffective, and full of unanswered requests because they have yet to learn how to cooperate with the Holy Spirit in prayer.

The only prayer life that will satisfy the spirit of the believer and accomplish Kingdom business is a supernatural prayer life; one that makes requests and receives answers; one that comes boldly to the throne and obtains; a prayer life that's based on the Word and cooperates with the Spirit of God; a prayer life where you are truly being a co-laborer with God.

God has made a supernatural prayer life available to His children; we have help in this great prayer life through the Person of the Holy Spirit.

Every person who is born again has the *indwelling* of the Spirit; for the Spirit of God bears witness with man's own spirit that he is a child of God. But once a man is born again, the additional privilege is offered to him of receiving the *infilling* of the Holy Spirit. When a man receives this infilling of the Holy Spirit, this is evidenced through speaking in tongues, for Acts 2:4 tells us:

And they were all FILLED with the Holy Ghost, and began to speak with other tongues, as the Spirit gave them utterance.

This great infilling of the Spirit is another dimension of God. To speak in other tongues is a supernatural action; it is a supernatural way to pray, for it requires the third Person of the Godhead to give us utterance.

The Spirit of God doesn't do the speaking; man does the speaking, but it's the Spirit who gives the utterances for man to speak.

Speaking in tongues enables man to have a supernatural prayer life. To the man who is filled with the Spirit and speaks in other tongues, he reaches into another realm in his prayer life. His prayer life isn't limited to himself, or to the mental arena that prays based only on human knowledge. The man who speaks in other tongues has the utterances of the Spirit of God on his lips, which carries the knowledge of God.

When a man prays from his mind, he only has his own knowledge to draw on. But the man who speaks forth utterances in other tongues given by the Holy Spirit draws on the knowledge of the Holy Spirit. We only know in part, but the Spirit has no limits to His knowledge. The Holy Spirit knows the mind of God, and the Spirit of God gives us utterances that are in line with the mind of God when we speak in other tongues.

To speak in other tongues is one of the greatest privileges given to God's children, but it is one of the most neglected privileges.

The enemy has done much to oppose, discredit and diminish the importance of speaking in other tongues because he's the one who suffers from it the most.

THE ROYAL TELEPHONE

First Corinthians 14:2 tells us:

For he that speaketh in an unknown tongue speaketh not unto men, but unto God: for no man understandeth him; howbeit in the spirit he speaketh mysteries.

When a man speaks in an unknown tongue in his private devotional life, he is not speaking to men, but to God. Man cannot understand him, for he is speaking God-talk. It's a communication that the enemy doesn't even understand. It's between the Father and His child.

With today's technology we have become so proud and amazed at ourselves for having advanced to small wireless cell phones that allow us to communicate with most anyone from most any location. But we have only a weak imitation of God's technology. He set up the first wireless form of communication over 2000 years ago on the Day of Pentecost. *"For he that speaketh in an unknown tongue speaketh not unto men, but unto God..."*

When we speak in an unknown tongue, we don't get an angel, we don't get a saint of old on the line – we get God Himself! To speak in tongues is to pick up the royal telephone and communicate firsthand with our Heavenly Father.

In the early 1990s, during the Desert Storm war, American reporters were sent to the war zone to interview the general who headed up the military at that time. The reporters took television cameras into the general's living quarters. In his room was a twin bed covered with a green army blanket, and a nightstand. On the nightstand was a lamp, a Bible and a red telephone. The reporter asked the general what the red telephone was for.

The general replied, "That's a direct line to the President of the United States." When he picked up that telephone, he didn't get a secretary, a presidential aide, an advisor, a congressman, or a senator, but he got the President of the United States on the line.

In a time of war, the general had to take direct orders from the President, who is the Commander and Chief of the armed forces, and that red telephone ensured him of a direct connection at a moment's notice in the face of an enemy attack.

Likewise, in the face of daily living or any pressing time, we have a royal telephone that allows us to communicate firsthand with our Heavenly Father. We can pick up that hotline to heaven anytime we want, and stay on the line for as long as we will, talking to our Father, allowing our spirit to fellowship with the Father of spirits.

On this royal telephone there are no party lines, dropped calls, or weak signals; we get God's undivided and full attention.

DIVINE MYSTERIES

To speak in other tongues is a divine ability that is to be an ongoing, vital part of the believer's everyday life; a divine flow in the believer's prayer life that satisfies the spirit of man and ushers him into the realm of the supernatural – the realm God intended for His children to live in.

The more we speak in other tongues, the more our lives will be filled with the supernatural.

First Corinthians 14:2 tells us:

For he that speaketh in an unknown tongue speaketh not unto men, but unto God: for no man understandeth him; howbeit in the spirit he speaketh MYSTERIES.

There is nothing that is a mystery to God; He has perfect understanding of all things. The mysteries lie with us. There are things that are a mystery to us about our own lives and the plan God has for us, but by taking time to speak in other tongues, we can tap into those mysteries, and gain the understanding we need so that we can make right steps and decisions in life that will steer us away from failure and into victory.

If you don't know which direction to take in an area of your life, take time to speak in other tongues. Give your spirit the opportunity to commune with the Father, the One who has all understanding, and as you speak in other tongues, He will impart His understanding to your own human spirit through the Person of the Holy Spirit. As you speak in other tongues, you are talking divine mysteries with your Father, and He is imparting His understanding to your own spirit. As your spirit receives understanding of what to do, that understanding floats up and enlightens your mind; then you'll know what to do.

If you don't know whether to enter into that business deal, buy that home, marry that person, or how to handle that difficulty with a child, if you will take time to speak in other tongues regarding that situation, you will get it clear in your spirit what to do. Then that understanding will float up and enlighten your mind, and the handling of that situation won't be a mystery to you anymore.

God does not intend that the mysteries concerning your life remain a mystery to you. He gave you this divine means of speaking in other tongues whereby you can tap into these mysteries, and move them from the arena of mysteries into the arena of revelation.

This is the invitation God extended to Jeremiah when He instructed him,

> *Call to Me and I will answer you and show you great and mighty things, fenced in and hidden, which you do not know (do not distinguish and recognize, have knowledge of and understand).*
> (Jeremiah 33:3, The Amplified Bible)

Doesn't the phrase "fenced in and hidden" sound a lot like the word "mysteries" used in First Corinthians 14:2?

We're invited to call unto God. How are we to call? The primary way we can do that is by speaking in other tongues. As we take time to speak in tongues regarding a situation, we are calling unto Him, and He will answer us. He will communicate His understanding to us, and we will receive light on what to do.

Where many people miss it, is they want prayer to do what only the Word will do for them. If God's Word is clear regarding your situation, you don't need to pray in tongues about that; you just need to be a doer of the Word.

In the details of your life, the Word may not give you specific instructions, but you can still know God's mind on those situations as you speak in tongues until you have clarity in your spirit of what you should do.

THE HOLY SPIRIT, OUR HELPER

First Corinthians 14:2 says that when you speak in other tongues, no man understands you; that would even include yourself; you don't even understand what you're saying. Then how do you know that you are praying for a particular need that is on your heart if you can't even understand what you're saying?

The Holy Spirit is called our Helper in John 14:16 (The Amplified Bible). He is not our doer. He only helps us in what we are doing.

For example, if I wanted to move a pulpit from one side of the sanctuary to the other side, but it was too heavy for me to move alone, I could ask an usher to come help me. If that usher stepped forward to help me move the pulpit, but I stepped back away from the pulpit a few feet, that usher would assume that I wasn't ready yet and wouldn't take hold of it. But if I move forward and lay hold of that pulpit, he would also move forward so he could help me move it. As my helper, the usher will help me to do what I am doing, but since he's not the doer, he won't do it apart from me.

Likewise, the Spirit is our Helper. He will help you do what you put your hand to. But since He is not the doer, He won't do it apart from you.

In lifting the pulpit to move it, if the usher was stronger than me, he would apply more strength than I could. Although he's my helper, we weren't equal in strength and he may actually lift more weight than me.

Even so, the strength of the Spirit is greater than our own human strength. We are to rely on the greatness of His strength and not on our own, but still we must initiate the doing, then He will help us to accomplish it, using His greater strength.

Now, if I wanted to move that pulpit and I ask the usher to help me, but he walks over and puts his hands on the sound monitor to move it, he's not helping me.

Even so, if you start speaking in other tongues concerning a certain situation, the Holy Spirit won't start giving you utterances for a different situation, or He wouldn't be helping you. No, He's going to put His hand to what you put your hand to. He's going to help you by picking up what you're picking up; otherwise, He's not being a Helper.

Many times, we think we're waiting on God to do something, when He is waiting on us to initiate something so the Holy Spirit can have something to help us with.

There are times the Spirit of God will prompt us in a certain direction, whether it be toward prayer, toward healing, toward giving, etc., but even then, He needs you to move that direction He's prompting you in so that He can help you. Without your obedience to that prompting, He can't do anything apart from you.

He may prompt you to pray, but if you don't pray, He can't help you. He may prompt you to exercise your faith for healing, but if you don't, He can't help you. He may prompt you to give, but if you don't give, He can't help you. He will be able to help you only as you do the doing.

No matter what the problem or situation may be in your life that is a mystery to you, you can know exactly what to do and how to handle it if you will take time to speak in other tongues, listen to what the Spirit of God says to your spirit, then act upon it.

PRAYER MOVES THE PLAN OF GOD FORWARD

I am in the ministry today because I took time to speak in other tongues. Although I knew I had a call to the ministry at the time I was born again at the age of 19, I got out of the will of God and was headed a direction other than what God had planned for me. I became so unhappy and so dissatisfied because I knew I wasn't in God's will.

You can have a call on your life, but you can miss out on fulfilling your ministry if you don't take time to wait before the Lord to know the specifics of your call, and to gain clarity in your spirit of His direction. One of the primary ways this is done is through praying in other tongues.

Some people think that because they're called that they will automatically qualify and fulfill their call, but they won't, "*...for many be called, but few chosen*" (Matthew 20:16). Few are chosen because few will separate themselves unto their call. Few will take the time to speak in tongues so that they can know the mysteries about their call and ministry. Few will take the time to wait before the Lord so they can know His will.

I knew that if I continued going the wrong direction, I would not fulfill the ministry God had for me.

I didn't know then what I know now. I didn't know the

great benefit of speaking in other tongues then, but I was unconsciously led by the Holy Spirit to separate myself daily to pray in other tongues – and I did.

After having spent hours a day speaking in other tongues for three weeks, the plan of God began to fall into place for my life.

I went to a church service one night, and it was there that I met my husband. Within a short time we were married, and I was thrust into the early stages of the ministry God had for me; I was back in the middle of God's will for my life.

All of that didn't come about because I was called to the ministry, and it didn't come about just because God had planned that for me all along; that came about because I took time to speak in other tongues.

Prayer helps move the plan of God forward. People don't move forward in the plan of God for their lives because they don't take time to pray in other tongues so that they can know what God's plan is for them.

What was once a mystery to me about what direction to go in life became a revelation because of the divine privilege of speaking in other tongues. Speaking in other tongues plays a major role in knowing and walking out God's plan for my life.

Christians create great difficulties for their own lives when they don't take time to speak in other tongues, and gain clarity from God in their spirits before moving forward in a particular direction. They marry the wrong people, get into bad business deals, make wrong career moves, allow wrong people around their children, and create a host of other problems for themselves, all because they don't take time to know the mysteries of God about their own lives through speaking in other tongues.

Do I always know exactly how to handle problems when faced with some of life's tests and circumstances? No, but I still know what to do. I take time to go aside with God, and speak in other tongues. I give my spirit the opportunity to fellowship with the God who understands all mysteries. He knows what I am to do, and He knows how to handle that difficulty; so, as I speak in other tongues my own spirit gains clarity. I can rest, knowing that nothing is a mystery to the One I'm in fellowship with.

Through the years, I have found that many people facing difficulties want relief, but they don't want to do what it takes to receive their help. When I've instructed them to take time to pray in tongues regarding their situation, they will excuse themselves from it by saying they don't have time. But I have always found that people will make time for what's important to them.

We don't have time to miss it! We don't have time to fail! We don't have time to make false steps and miss the mark! Therefore, we must take time to speak in other tongues; we must take time to know the mysteries of God about our life so that we can live accurately and with the right purpose.

Let's not neglect this supernatural means of communicating with God. Let's take advantage of this divine privilege.

THE MIND OF GOD

The Amplified Bible in First Corinthians 14:2 reads:

For one who speaks in an [unknown] tongue speaks not to men but to God, for no one understands or catches his meaning, because in the [Holy] Spirit he utters SECRET TRUTHS and hidden things [not obvious to the understanding].

Another translation says, *"He talks DIVINE SECRETS."*

When a believer speaks in tongues, he touches into an area of the divine that he would have never accessed otherwise. Believers have a royal invitation to partake of the divine secrets and mysteries that belong to God.

Where are these divine secrets and mysteries kept? They are contained in the mind of God. And the Spirit of God, who knows the mind of God, helps us to access and partake of these great secrets and mysteries contained in the mind of God; for as we speak in other tongues, the utterances that the Spirit gives us ushers us into these divine secrets.

God is looking for those who long to know the secrets and the mysteries that are held in His mind. He longs to fellowship with His children on this level, which is His level – Spirit to spirit.

Those who will take time to commune with Him through speaking in other tongues will have granted to them an entrance into these secret truths and divine secrets. These mysteries of God that will bring to our lives divine revelation, divine understanding, and divine knowledge.

As we take time to speak in other tongues, the spirit of "seeing and knowing" will flow in a stronger way; we will see what God sees, and know what He knows about different situations. We will then partake of the divine flow in a deeper way.

AN OUTPOURING OF KNOWLEDGE

It is no happy coincidence that the mightiest strides in technology and inventions were made after the great Azusa Street Revival of the early 1900s, which brought the infilling of the Holy Ghost with the evidence of speaking in other tongues to the forefront.

From the time of Adam until the early 1900s, man's mode of transportation remained virtually unchanged. He either walked or rode horses, wagons, or bicycles of some sort.

But when the truth of being filled with the Holy Ghost with the evidence of speaking in other tongues came to the forefront through the Azusa Street Revival, man began to cooperate with God in a deeper dimension. With an outpouring of the Spirit, there came an outpouring of knowledge.

There were not just pockets on the earth where men embraced the infilling of the Holy Spirit with the evidence of speaking in other tongues, as in times past, but this divine blessing of speaking in other tongues spread worldwide, to every nation. Then, through speaking in other tongues, men everywhere began to access the mind of God, where the divine mysteries and secrets are contained, and one result was that the inventions of man began to tap into another arena.

Man was no longer limited to walking and riding slow means of transportation, as he had done since the time of Adam; but now he was riding cars, jets and rockets. Wireless communications have since come into place, and computer technology has opened up a whole new arena of existence to man.

These giant strides in technology came about as man, on a worldwide scale, began to access the divine secrets and mysteries contained in the mind of God.

IMPACTED BY THE SPIRIT

If the emphasis of speaking in other tongues impacts the world of technology, which is in this temporal realm, just think what it would mean to the personal, spiritual life of every believer.

There is an unseen, eternal realm, the realm of God, that we can access, which contains all the blessings of God. Speaking in other tongues is one means whereby we access that all-conquering realm. That's the realm of blessing, that's the realm of all authority, that's the realm of all possibilities. No impossibilities exist in that realm. Impossibilities are unknown in that realm.

Let's cooperate with the Spirit of God. Let's allow Him a greater flow through us, allowing Him to give us these mighty utterances in other tongues.

The more we pray in the Spirit, the farther we'll go in the spirit.

Let's not be content to just stay in the outer fringes of the spiritual life. Let's give ourselves the spiritual habit and lifestyle of speaking in other tongues. Let's delve deeper into the dimension of God that is available to us through speaking in other tongues.

CHAPTER FOUR

Living Full of the Spirit

Living full of the Spirit is the only way to accomplish living in its highest sense. It is the only way to be the supply God intended for us to be. To live and minister in the power of the Spirit is the only kind of life and ministry that will finish its course.

The life of Smith Wigglesworth was earmarked by the fullness of the Spirit and the flow of the supernatural. Following are some of his quotes that give us insight into his life in the Spirit.

"Only one thing will meet the needs of the people, and that is for you to be immersed in the life of God."

"If you find me on the street or anywhere else, if I am alone, I will be talking to God. I make it my business to talk to God all the time. If I wake in the night, I make it my business to pray. I believe that's the reason God keeps me right, always right, always ready."

"I have revival everywhere I go because I live full of the Spirit."

"Nothing is impossible to a man filled with the Holy Spirit."

"Being filled with the Spirit is worthwhile, no matter what it costs!"

"I see anything not done in the Spirit as failure."

Ephesians 3:19, (The Amplified Bible) tells us how every child of God is to live,

> *...so that you may be FILLED [through all your being] unto all the FULLNESS of God [MAY HAVE THE RICHEST MEASURE OF THE DIVINE PRESENCE, AND BECOME A BODY WHOLLY FILLED AND FLOODED WITH GOD HIMSELF]!*

Anything less than full is to have a lesser measure of God than He offers. To be filled with the Spirit is to move into another dimension of God.

After Jesus had been raised from the dead, He appeared to His disciples and instructed them that they were to go to Jerusalem and wait there until they received the gift of the Holy Spirit. Once this divine Person was sent to the earth to dwell in man, they would become spiritual supermen; they would be able to accomplish works of power that would mark them as co-laborers with God. With this great infilling of the Holy Spirit, every region of the earth would feel the impact as they cooperated with this mighty One.

We see in Jesus' own earthly ministry that no sermons were preached, no miracles were worked, and no healings occurred until the Person of the Holy Spirit descended upon Jesus in the form of a dove at His baptism (Luke 3:21 & 22).

Luke 4:1 tells us, *"And Jesus being FULL of the Holy Ghost returned from Jordan, and was LED by the Spirit..."* We see here that because Jesus was full, He was also led; there is a connection between being full of the Spirit, and being led of the Spirit.

44

A full person is easily led. A full man lives yielded to God. It's the full man who more readily knows and perceives the leading of God. An empty man stumbles around in difficulty, wondering which way to go, making false steps all along the way. Many Christians, who haven't taken the time to live full of the Spirit, endeavor to follow their spirits, but get lost, because you must be full to know His leadings. Problems in life come when living on empty.

It is the full-time occupation of the believer to live full of the Word and the Spirit. Anything less will mean unnecessary hardships.

Living full of the Word and the Spirit is the only way to live ready. Many don't move forward in God because they're not ready when opportunities come. But if we'll live full of the Spirit, the Spirit will always keep us ready for all that's ahead of us.

How do we live full of the Spirit? Acts 2:4 tells us,

> *And they were all FILLED with the Holy Ghost, and began to SPEAK WITH OTHER TONGUES, as the Spirit gave them utterance.*

The initial evidence of being full of the Spirit was that they spoke in other tongues. To live full of the Spirit, speak in other tongues.

It is not God's responsibility to keep us full of the Spirit, it is ours! He has given us the means whereby we can live full of the Spirit, but it is up to us to stir ourselves up and fill ourselves up through speaking in other tongues.

KNOW THE WILL OF GOD

Ephesians 5:17 & 18 instructs us, *"Wherefore be ye not unwise, but understanding what the will of the Lord is...be filled with the Spirit."*

It is the will of God that all of His children be filled with the Spirit. Why? Because it's only those who are filled that can be continually led by Him.

The Amplified Bible of Ephesians 5:15 & 17 tells us:

Look carefully then how you walk! Live purposefully and worthily and accurately, not as the unwise and witless, but as wise...Therefore do not be vague and thoughtless and foolish, but understanding and firmly grasping what the will of the Lord is.

These verses of scripture tell us that those who are filled with the Spirit are the ones who will understand what the will of the Lord is for their life.

Empty people lack understanding. Empty people lack the knowledge of God's will for their lives. Empty people are difficult for God or man to lead.

Living full of the Spirit is the condition for God's perfect and unhindered working in us and through us. The benefits of His fullness reach into our future and bless it.

IN THE SPIRIT, OUR WAY OF LIFE

Under the Old Covenant, the only ones who had the Holy Spirit were the prophet, the priest, and the king, but no others under that covenant had the Holy Spirit. They couldn't pray with the same ability we can pray with. They couldn't worship God in the same fullness that we can.

Under the New Covenant, God emphasizes being filled with the Spirit. We are to walk in the Spirit, live in the Spirit, pray in the Spirit, and worship in the Spirit. As Smith Wigglesworth stated, "I see anything not done in the Spirit as failure." If we don't walk in the Spirit, we will miss the mark. Without walking in the Spirit, our ministries won't succeed and reach their full potential. Without walking in the Spirit, we're only left to live out of our minds and our flesh.

But we are warned in Ephesians 4:17 (The Amplified Bible),

> *So this I say and solemnly testify in [the name of] the Lord [as in His presence], that you must no longer live as the heathen (the Gentiles) do in their perverseness [in the folly, vanity, and EMPTINESS of their souls and the FUTILITY] OF THEIR MINDS.*

Life is futile when it's lived out of the mental arena. God has given us a better way to live, a higher way to live, a more accurate way to live; we are to live full of the Spirit!

BE DRUNK ON THE SPIRIT

Notice that Ephesians 5:18 warns us, "*And be not drunk with wine, wherein is excess...*" Those who drink wine will slip into an excess that brings great harm and damage. As they drink it, they damage and kill the body, and they destroy lives around them. Alcohol has never blessed any life; the excess it carries with it is destructive. Any Christian who drinks alcohol is letting you know that he is empty of the Spirit, and he is trying to fill himself with something natural, but he will suffer the consequences.

The reason any unsaved man ever drinks is because he can't face life sober; there are too many heartbreaks and heartaches he's facing.

But God didn't intend that His children live life sober either! He instructs us to be filled, be drunk, with the Spirit!

When a man drinks alcohol, the excess that comes with it is destructive, for we're told,

> *And be not drunk with wine, wherein is excess; but*
> *BE FILLED WITH THE SPIRIT (WHEREIN*
> *THERE IS NO EXCESS).*

There is no limit to the fullness of the Spirit! You can drink and drink and drink, and there is no limit to how much you can have. No matter how great a measure you drink of the Spirit, there is nothing that will harm or destroy you. It will only cause you to be more full of God!

PSALMS, HYMNS AND SPIRITUAL SONGS

Ephesians 5:18 tells us, *"And be not drunk with wine, wherein is excess; but BE FILLED with the Spirit."* Greek scholars tell us that a more accurate translation of the phrase *"be filled with the Spirit"* actually reads, *"BE BEING FILLED with the Spirit."* The Amplified Bible shows this as well, for it says, *"but EVER BE FILLED and stimulated with the [Holy] Spirit."* Both of these phrases denote an ongoing, continual action that we must take.

How are we to continually be filled with the Spirit?

BE (BEING) *FILLED WITH THE SPIRIT; SPEAKING to yourselves in psalms and hymns and spiritual songs, SINGING and making melody in your heart to the Lord.*

(Ephesians 5:18-19)

We are continually filled with the Spirit as we speak to ourselves in psalms, hymns, and spiritual songs, and as we sing and make melody in our hearts to the Lord.

We hold ourselves in the spirit realm through speaking with psalms, hymns, and spiritual songs, and through singing songs that come from our spirits. When faced with opposition and trials, you can hold yourself in the spirit realm through these methods.

In past years, the Spirit of God has brought light to the body of Christ on the necessity and the benefits of speaking to ourselves in psalms, hymns, and spiritual songs. We must hold fast to the light that we gained so that we don't let it slip.

A *psalm* is a spiritual poem or ode. It may rhyme or it may not; however, there is an element of poetry about it. It may be sung, chanted, or just recited.

The Old Testament contains 150 Psalms, most of which were written by David. These psalms were given to him by the inspiration of the Holy Spirit to benefit him in his daily life, and as he faced difficult times in life.

A *hymn* is a song of praise and worship addressed to and directed toward God.

A *spiritual song* is a song that brings forth the revelation of the Word that the Holy Spirit has given you.

Psalms, hymns, and spiritual songs are given by the Holy Spirit, and they're "hot off the wire" from heaven. These are supernatural utterances that the Holy Spirit gives at the spur of the moment by the spirit of prophecy. The simple gift of prophecy *"speaketh unto men to edification, and exhortation, and comfort."* (It is not to be confused with the prophet's office, which often gives revelation of the future.) To prophesy is to speak in a known tongue under the inspiration of the Holy Spirit, and it will edify, exhort and comfort (First Corinthians 14:3). Every believer is to be speaking these forth in his private devotional life.

Speaking in other tongues is the door that helps us to enter into speaking in psalms, hymns, and spiritual songs.

As we speak to ourselves in psalms, hymns, and spiritual songs, we open the way for God's wisdom and knowledge to flow, and we can receive instructions for living.

Colossians 3:16 is a companion verse to Ephesians 5:19, reading,

> *Let the word of Christ dwell in you richly in all wisdom; TEACHING AND ADMONISHING ONE ANOTHER in psalms and hymns and spiritual songs, singing with grace in your hearts to the Lord.*

This verse shows us that we can even have the flow of psalms, hymns and spiritual songs operating in our church services which will edify, exhort and comfort those present.

As we speak to ourselves in psalms, hymns and spiritual songs, we are worshipping God in Spirit and truth, we are

50

edifying ourselves, we are kept mindful of the greater One within us and we keep ourselves full of the Spirit.

The New Testament places much emphasis on living a life full of the Spirit, so we must also emphasize it in our daily lives.

CHAPTER FIVE

Quieting the Mind

A believer can speak in other tongues, but not fully benefit from it if he doesn't learn to first, quiet his mind, and second, focus on his spirit while speaking in other tongues.

To quiet the mind is to put the mind in neutral, not thinking on anything in particular, or to think on the Lord Jesus.

The mind is so used to getting all the movement that it fights to keep all the movement. Speaking in other tongues is not a mental exercise, but a spiritual exercise; your spirit is to get the movement as you speak in other tongues.

As you practice quieting the mind while speaking in other tongues, and focus on your spirit, you will be allowing your spirit to gain the movement, and you'll be able to more readily perceive what the Lord is saying to your own spirit.

When God speaks to you, the Spirit communicates what God is saying to your spirit; then in turn, what the Spirit of God says to your spirit will float up and enlighten your mind. But if your mind is busy, occupied with other thoughts, your mind will miss what your spirit is saying, and you won't gain the full benefit of speaking in other tongues.

No, God doesn't speak to your mind, He speaks to your spirit; but your spirit will enlighten your mind. God doesn't communicate with you on a mental level. He is a Spirit, and He made you a spirit being; therefore, He will communicate with you through your spirit.

Man is a spirit, he has a soul (made up of the mind, the will, and the emotions), and he lives in a body. The most important feature of man is not his mind or his body, but his spirit.

Proverbs 20:27 tells us, *"The spirit of man is the candle of the Lord."* This means that God is going to enlighten you through your spirit; He's going to speak to you through your spirit. God is not a mind; He doesn't communicate with man on a mental level. God is a Spirit, and He made man a spirit being; He made man in His own image. Since we are spirit beings, God can communicate with man on His own level – Spirit to spirit.

DEVELOP YOUR SPIRIT

Since the spirit of man is the most important feature of man, it's to be regretted that many believers have never taken the time to develop their spirits.

Many have developed their minds through education, and developed their bodies through exercise, but have neglected to exercise their spirits, leaving them spiritually weak and feeble. That's why many don't hear when God speaks to them, or don't perceive when He's moving; they are spiritually undeveloped and dull.

But the believer is to develop and exercise his spirit so that his fellowship with the Lord will be rich, and the fruit of his life abundant.

How does one develop their spirit? The Word of God is food for the spirit of man. If a man is to be physically strong, he must eat the right food. Likewise, if a believer is to be spiritually strong, he must feed his spirit the right food, which is the Word of God.

Not only must the believer feed his spirit, but he must also exercise his spirit.

How does a believer exercise his spirit? By being a doer of the Word, by acting on the Word.

If a man eats food, but never exercises his body, he will become unhealthy. Likewise, if a man feeds his spirit on the Word of God, but fails to act on that Word, he will become spiritually unhealthy; for acting on the Word does for man's spirit what physical exercise does for man's body.

Another key way for man to develop his spirit is to speak in other tongues, for Jude 20 tells us,

> *But ye, beloved, BUILDING UP YOURSELVES* (your spirit) *on your most holy faith, praying in the Holy Ghost* (praying in other tongues).

When you pray in other tongues, you are giving your spirit the privilege of fellowshipping with your Heavenly Father, and you're communing with Him on His level – a spiritual level.

Take time to speak in other tongues; it is a primary way to develop your own human spirit, and a primary way to distinguish the voice of God.

HEARING THE SPIRIT

Since God speaks to you through your spirit, it is imperative that you learn to quiet the mind so that you can hear your spirit.

Someone may say, "I don't know what it means to quiet the mind," but I dare to say that when you watch television, that's what you're doing – quieting the mind. Yes, you are watching what's on the television, but your mind isn't actively thinking in any particular direction. That's why many will turn on the television at the end of a long, busy day; so they can unwind, and relax mentally and physically.

It may take some time of practice to quiet the mind, but the more you practice, the better and the quicker you get at it.

As you speak in other tongues, quiet your mind and focus on your spirit. As you focus on your spirit, you will perceive the movement of your own spirit.

Jesus declared in John 7:38, "...*out of his BELLY shall flow rivers of living water*." He was speaking of those who are filled with the Holy Ghost.

Out of your belly you will sense the movement of the Spirit of God within your own spirit as you speak in other tongues; you will sense the flow of life moving in your spirit. Focus on that flow. Shut out everything else.

If I seem to have an unusually hard time quieting my mind as I speak in other tongues, I will speak to my mind to be quiet in Jesus' Name. My mind is under the control of my spirit, so I take authority over it.

56

It's crucial that the believer learn to quiet their mind as they speak in other tongues so that their spirit can enlighten their mind. That's the only way to understand what God is saying to you.

Those who have rutted themselves in a mental way of living may have to practice quieting the mind, but it's imperative for spiritual development. You won't learn to do it overnight, but as you practice it more and more, it will become easier and easier.

The more you handle a situation in the mental arena, the harder it can be for you to discern God's leading. Some people faced with a decision will handle it so much in the mental arena, endeavoring to figure it out, that the noise of their own mind drowns out what their spirit is saying to them. Take time to quiet the mind, let go of what you have figured out, and hear what the Spirit would say to you as you take time to speak in other tongues and focus on your spirit.

Some Christians live such mental lives, but they are cheating themselves from the supernatural way of living that God intended for them.

CHAPTER SIX

Edifying Yourself

Speaking in tongues is for your private devotional use, but it is also for public use in the church. First Corinthians 14 is a chapter that teaches us about tongues for private devotional use, and for public use.

Someone may read statements Paul writes in First Corinthians 14 and think that Paul is laying little stress on speaking in tongues, but Paul is simply instructing that in public, you should bring edification, exhortation and comfort to those present, and so people must understand what's being said for that to be accomplished. Therefore, speaking in tongues, but not interpreting it, wouldn't bring edification, exhortation or comfort to the people because they wouldn't understand what's being said.

Paul was used by the Spirit of God to bring the greatest amount of revelation to the church, other than Jesus. But I believe he gives us insight as to how he came to possess so much divine revelation; he declared, *"I thank my God, I speak with tongues more than ye all."* The Amplified Bible states,

> *I thank God that I speak in [strange] tongues (languages) MORE THAN ANY OF YOU OR ALL OF YOU PUT TOGETHER.*
>
> (First Corinthians 14:18)

Through this scripture, we can see that Paul laid great emphasis on speaking in other tongues in his private devotional life.

In First Corinthians 14:4, we are instructed, *"He that speaketh in an unknown tongue EDIFIETH himself."* Paul is letting us know that as we speak in other tongues in our own private devotional life, we edify ourselves.

The Amplified Bible of this same verse reads, *"He who speaks in a [strange] tongue EDIFIES AND IMPROVES HIMSELF."* Speaking in other tongues improves you!

Notice who is responsible for your edification – you are! It's not God's job to edify you. He has given you the means whereby you can be edified, through speaking in other tongues, but it's up to you to do the speaking in other tongues; it's not even up to the Holy Spirit – it's up to you. The Holy Spirit doesn't do the speaking in other tongues – you do. The Holy Spirit gives you the utterances, but you're the one who has to speak out those utterances. So, whether or not you're edified depends on you.

Smith Wigglesworth, a minister from England who was mightily used of God in the first half of the 1900's, commented that before he would go out to preach, he would lie on his bed and speak in other tongues to edify himself, then he'd go out and edify the people.

Edified people edify others. Un-edified people edify no one.

You don't have to have God compel you or move on you before you speak in other tongues. You don't have to sense a special anointing on you before you speak in other tongues; you can speak in other tongues at will. Anytime you want, you can edify yourself through speaking in other tongues.

Look at what Paul writes in First Corinthians 14:15:

I WILL pray with the spirit (in other tongues)*, and I WILL pray with the understanding* (in my known language).

Notice that Paul writes *"I WILL."* We can speak in tongues as we will. We don't have to wait for a special anointing or unction to come upon us before we speak in other tongues. The Holy Spirit is ever present in us, so He is ever present to give us utterances. We can yield to the utterance He gives any time we will, and speak out those utterances in other tongues. The Bible tells us what will happen when we do – we edify and improve ourselves.

When you speak in other tongues, the part of you that's edified is your spirit, but once your spirit is edified, it can't help but have a positive effect on your mind and body.

When you take time to speak in other tongues, you make yourself spirit conscious; and when you're more spirit conscious, your mind loses dominion, and your body loses dominion. When your life becomes ruled by your spirit instead of by your mind and body, life is improved, your walk with God is improved, and everything connected with your life is improved, for he that speaks in an unknown tongue improves himself.

The difficulties that used to plague your mind and body will lose their grip as you speak in other tongues, for you will become more spirit conscious, more God-inside minded.

Difficulties will seem less formidable to the one who takes time to edify and improve himself through speaking in tongues.

Tongues for edification is a much neglected privilege in the lives of many believers, but if believers would take the time to partake of this divine privilege, their lives would show the edification and improvement that comes through speaking in other tongues.

TONGUES FOR EDIFICATION

It's important to state that speaking in tongues for the purpose of edification shouldn't be confused with other kinds of prayer.

When speaking in other tongues for the purpose of edification, you're not occupying your mind with anything, or praying about someone else's situation, but you're praying for the benefit of your own spiritual welfare.

When you're speaking in other tongues for the purpose of edification, it's important to quiet the mind and focus on your spirit so that your spirit can enlighten your mind, for that's when you're edified and improved.

It's good and right to meditate on God's Word, but when speaking in other tongues for the purpose of edification, it's best to quiet the mind; for when you're meditating on scriptures, the mind is busy and occupied, and you could miss what your spirit is trying to communicate to your mind.

It is good, right, and appropriate to meditate on the Word and speak in other tongues at the same time; but that's called meditation. But speaking in other tongues for the purpose of edification involves the mind being quieted so you can hear what your spirit would say.

Now, don't misunderstand me. When you are speaking in other tongues, scriptures may float up to your mind and a revelation of God's Word may come to you in a way that you've never seen before; God is enlightening you by revelation of His Word, and that will edify you. But in that instance, the scripture comes up from your spirit and enlightens your mind, as opposed to the mind just randomly grabbing a scripture and meditating on it.

When you're praying in other tongues for the purpose of edification, you're quieting your mind and focusing on your spirit, but it's during that time that answers and enlightenment of the Word will float up to your mind, and when that happens, you're edified.

When a man takes time to speak in other tongues for the purpose of edifying and improving himself, that man won't stay the same; life will be different for him, for he has employed the supernatural. No man's life remains untouched when the supernatural gift of speaking in other tongues is made a priority in the life of a man.

I'M MY GREATEST DIFFICULTY!

John Wesley, who was the founder of the Methodist church, made a mighty impact on this earth. Throughout his many years of ministry, he was faced with much persecution and hardship, but at the close of his life, thousands and thousands had been affected by his ministry.

He had thousands of ministers who were under his leadership and looked to him as an example to follow.

In his latter years, a group of ministers gathered and asked him questions. Knowing the severe, life-threatening persecutions and attacks John Wesley had faced, one young minister asked him, "What has been your greatest difficulty in life?"

John Wesley quickly replied, "Oh, that's easy. Me! I've been my greatest difficulty!"

Really, every believer's greatest difficulty is himself. Satan isn't our greatest difficulty, for Jesus spoiled principalities and powers and made a show of their defeat openly (Colossians 2:15).

Other people aren't our greatest difficulty, for we don't have to answer for their actions; we will only have to answer for our own actions. We aren't anointed to change anyone but ourselves. We are anointed to tell others what the Word offers for their lives, but they're the only ones who can make any needed changes.

No, we are our biggest problem. Wrong thinking, wrong believing, wrong words, wrong attitudes, and wrong actions all serve to have a negative affect on our lives.

But the good news is that we can improve ourselves. We can edify ourselves. We can get past ourselves as we take time to renew our mind with the Word of God, act on that Word, and take time to speak in other tongues.

Those faults and shortcomings that are present with every man can be dealt with. The personal quirks that we may have that we dislike about our own selves can be minimized, overshadowed and improved as we take time to speak in other tongues.

It's our personal quirks, shortcomings, and frailties that cause us to bump into other people, and offer offense to others, but we don't have to stay the way we are. We can be edified and improved.

Believers who have taken the time to edify and improve themselves are the most desirable people to be around.

As we speak in other tongues, the spirit of man, which houses the power and life of God, becomes the most dominant feature about our lives, and all men seek out the company of such a man.

Men are hungry for the company of a man of the Spirit, a God-filled man, a spirit-dominated man. All the world is drawn to a full man!

What you're full of will determine what kind of man will be drawn to you. Those full of rebellion draw the rebellious. Those full of fear draw the fearful.

Those full of pride draw the prideful. But those full of faith, full of the Spirit, full of God, draw like men.

No Self-Help Will Do

The Holy Spirit is the great Helper. He helps us by giving us the utterance whereby a man can edify and improve himself. No need for the self-help resources and methods natural-minded men resort to.

The Lord is our Helper! The Lord is the strength of our lives! We're edified, we're improved as we fill our mouths with divine utterances in other tongues. Take time to do your part by speaking forth those utterances.

Don't spend your days in idle, unprofitable, unimportant, mental living. Don't keep your spirit imprisoned by living a carnal, mental, natural existence, but allow your spirit to gain movement. Allow the divine a place in your life. Flow with the supernatural. Edify and improve yourself. Give yourself the daily spiritual habit and lifestyle of speaking in other tongues.

CHAPTER SEVEN

Edifying Defined

The insight the Holy Spirit gives to us through Paul rings loud in my spirit. *"He that speaketh in an unknown tongue EDIFIETH (IMPROVES) himself"* (First Corinthians 14:4).

In looking in Webster's Dictionary for definitions given for the word "edify," I found several definitions. (When Daniel Webster first wrote the dictionary, he used many Bible scriptures for his definitions, and he referenced those scriptures in his definitions. But over time and multiple printings, many of those scripture references have been edited out of the later printings. My copy is an earlier printing from the 1800's that's about 12 inches thick, and it contains those scriptural references.)

#1 – THE FIRE OF GOD

Let's look at the definitions given for the word "edify".

1) kindle – He that speaks in an unknown tongue kindles himself.

To kindle a fire is to ignite a fire, and throw wood on it to keep it burning.

He that speaks in an unknown tongue ignites the fire of God, and keeps himself burning hot for God; he doesn't become lukewarm in his fellowship with God or in his labor with God.

You may remember Revelation 3:15 & 16, (The Amplified Bible) that speaks about one of the seven churches. Jesus addressed the Laodicean church, telling them,

> *...you are neither cold nor hot. Would that you were cold or hot! So, because you are lukewarm and neither cold nor hot, I will spew you out of My mouth.*

In this passage, Jesus speaks of being spiritually cold as better than being spiritually lukewarm. At first, we might not understand that; we would assume that being spiritually lukewarm would be better than being spiritually cold. But we have to consider, how did something become lukewarm? It once had heat applied to it, but the heat was removed, and it lost its fire.

Jesus is saying that He would rather that one be spiritually cold, meaning they never had the fire of God, than to be lukewarm, meaning they had a measure of God's fire, but cut it off.

He that speaks in an unknown tongue will keep the fire of God moving in his life. He will keep the inner fire burning hot for God.

Second Timothy 1:6 tells us, *"STIR UP the GIFT of God."* To be filled with the Holy Spirit with the evidence of speaking in other tongues is a gift of God.

The Amplified Bible of Second Timothy 1:6 reads,

> *I would remind you to STIR UP (REKINDLE the embers of, fan the flame of, and KEEP BURNING)*

*the [gracious] gift of God, [THE INNER FIRE] that
is in you.*

How do we keep the fire of God, the gift of God, stirred
up? One way is through speaking in other tongues, for *"He
that speaketh in an unknown tongue edifieth* (kindles) *himself."*

SERVING WITH THE FIRE OF GOD

He that speaks in an unknown tongue also kindles himself in the ministry God has called him to; he keeps himself
burning hot in the direction God has called him to go.

A man who takes time to speak in other tongues won't
become unfaithful in his ministry. A man who takes time
to speak in other tongues won't become bored with the ministry he's called to; out of boredom he won't start wandering
into an office that God didn't call him to, which is something
that must be guarded against.

A believer who speaks in other tongues keeps himself
hot in serving in his ministry of helps position in the local
church. He won't become bored and unfaithful in his service, but his own serving will be an example for others to follow, igniting them in their service with the Lord.

Speaking in other tongues will keep a man hot for God
in every arena of life, and keep him ignited for God's purpose and plan.

All God has provided for us flows freely and easily for
the one whose fellowship and service with God is burning
hot. Speaking in tongues plays a vital role in maintaining
that spiritual glow.

Bringing Forth Young

In looking up the definition for the word "kindle," I found a definition that surprised me. One definition for *"kindle"* is *"to bring forth young."*

Isaiah 66:8 tells us, *"for as soon as Zion* (the church) *travailed, she brought forth her children."*

We can see that through the help of the Holy Spirit, we can speak forth divine utterances, which plays a role in bringing forth spiritual children. Speaking in tongues plays a role in spiritual babies being born into the kingdom of God; it makes power available to those who need to receive salvation.

No, prayer doesn't save people. Jesus is the Savior who has already accomplished His saving work. But as we cooperate with the Holy Spirit in prayer, the power of God that's offered to every man for salvation will flow and make it easier for people to make the right decision to receive the salvation Jesus provided for them.

#2 – Building Your Spirit

Let's look at the next definition Webster gave for the word "edify."

2) build – He that speaks in an unknown tongue builds himself.

Smith Wigglesworth made the statement, "I'm a thousand times bigger on the inside than I am on the outside." He was saying that his spirit was so much larger than his body; and his life showed the fruit of that enlargement.

Thousands of miracles, healings, and works of divine power flowed from his large spirit.

Speaking in tongues plays a vital role in building a man's spirit. An enlarged spirit has an enlarged capacity for God's power and ability.

You can hear the largeness of a man's spirit who walks with God. His words sound different, they carry a weightiness. His words of power and revelation will seem to strike a chord in your own spirit. His words will land in you with such force and power, and they won't leave you in the place they found you.

He that speaks in an unknown tongue edifies (builds) himself. It takes longer to build something than it does to tear it down. It takes more effort to build but it is effort in a positive direction. It is a longer process, but the results of it are worthwhile. Building your own spirit is worth whatever it costs.

The building process that takes place in a man through speaking in other tongues won't happen overnight, but if he's faithful to make it a lifestyle, he will make giant strides in his spiritual life, and his progress will be apparent to all those around him.

In Psalm 127:1, God gives us a warning: *"Except the Lord build the house, they labour in vain that build it."* The "house" can refer to a man's spirit, a man's life, a man's ministry, and a man's purpose. God warns us that it must be by His ability that all these are built; not by mental ability, physical ability, or education's ability, but by God-given spiritual ability.

Notice in Psalm 127:1, that the house got built but it was built by vain labor; therefore, it's a work done in vain. It will never produce all the fruit that could have been produced had the Lord been the builder. It was built apart from the Lord's ability; man's mental and physical ability was its supply, and it fell short.

When building any facet or arena of our life, we must employ the supernatural. When we take time to speak in other tongues, we are employing supernatural, divine help; we are cooperating with our divine Helper, and we are tapping into the thoughts and plans of God, and utilizing His almightiness. What a building it will become! What a place of glory, honor and power for our Father to flow through!

The building of a man's spirit, his life, ministry and purpose is not to be done by human, natural might and power, but by His Spirit, the ability and power that proceeds from God. God has given us this great divine Helper to ensure our success in the building process; and we utilize His help as we speak forth the utterance He gives us in other tongues.

As a wife, a mother, a minister, a teacher, a pastor, I can only build in these areas successfully as I do them by the Spirit, relying on the help the Spirit gives. *"Not by might, nor by power, but by my spirit"* (Zechariah 4:6).

PREPARING TO MINISTER

As a minister, a teacher, and a pastor, I spend my hours prior to ministering sitting quietly and speaking in other tongues. Before I can edify the people, I must be edified.

I study God's Word daily as a part of my lifestyle; and by speaking in other tongues, I can best draw the truths of the Word out of my own spirit that will feed those who will be present in the service. So, I spend the few hours prior to the service hooking my tongue up to my spirit through speaking in other tongues.

Then, when I minister to the people, I minister out of my spirit, as opposed to out of my head; then the Word ministered will reach deep into the spirit of those who are hearing, and won't fall short by just landing in their heads.

TONGUES IS THE DOOR TO THE GIFTS OF THE SPIRIT

Speaking in other tongues is the door to the supernatural. It is the spiritual action that ushers us in to operating in the gifts of the Spirit that flow as the Spirit wills. We aren't the ones who decide when and how the nine gifts of the Spirit flow and operate; they flow only as the Spirit wills. But through speaking in other tongues, we make our spirits sensitive to the Holy Spirit, and we put ourselves in the position to perceive when He wants to manifest Himself through one of the nine gifts.

Those who take time to speak much in other tongues will have more gifts of the Spirit flowing in their daily lives and through their ministry than those who don't speak much in other tongues.

John 16:13 tells us that the Spirit of God will show us things to come. The more we take time to speak in other tongues, the more God will be able to show us things to come.

I have had many wonderful experiences with God in prayer as a result of taking time to speak in other tongues. Tragedies have been averted, and lives have been spared.

By taking the time to speak in other tongues, God has shown me things about my own life, things about the lives of our children, things about the ministry we're called to, and He has also shown me things that have helped the lives of other people.

BABY'S LIFE SPARED

One such incident occurred as I was speaking in other tongues before I fell off to sleep one night.

As I lay in bed speaking quietly in other tongues, I saw a one-year old boy with a very unsteady walk wander onto a driveway and stop behind a silver truck. While he was standing there, I saw a man climb into the truck and, not knowing the baby was behind him, back over the child.

When I saw that, I said, "I bind the spirit of death from off that child in Jesus' Name, and I loose the power of God and the angels of God to protect him."

I continued to pray in other tongues for a short time, but I sensed a release, so I fell off to sleep.

When God showed me that child being run over, He didn't just show it to me so that I could say I saw it. He showed it to me so that I would exercise my authority over it, and get it changed.

We have authority over the enemy, and we can abort his plans.

When God put Adam on the earth, He gave Adam dominion over the earth. It was Adam's job to guard, protect and tend the earth (Genesis 1:28).

When Adam failed to exercise his authority and keep Satan out of the garden, he yielded to the enemy, sinned against God and committed high treason. The authority that once belonged to Adam, Adam turned over to Satan; then Satan became the god of this world (First Corinthians 4:4).

But when Jesus defeated Satan, He spoiled principalities and powers. He made a show of their defeat openly (Colossians 2:15). He took from Satan the authority that had once belonged to Adam, and gave it back to man.

Jesus told us of our restored authority when He declared,

Behold, I give unto you power (authority) to tread on serpents and scorpions, and over all the power of the enemy: and nothing shall by any means hurt you.
(Luke 10:19)

The Word tells us that whatsoever we bind shall be bound, and whatsoever we loose shall be loosed, because we have authority (Matthew 16:19).

We are co-laborers with God. God's part was to supply the authority and the power, but our part is to *exercise* the power and authority. If we don't exercise our authority over the devil, it won't get exercised.

God allows what we allow. God permits what we permit.

Some Christians are waiting on God to do something with the devil, but since Jesus gave us authority, we are the ones who must exercise authority over him on this earth.

God showed me that child being run over by the truck so that I would exercise my authority over the situation, and the child's life could be saved.

Although I was praying in other tongues when I saw that happen to the child, I don't use other tongues to deal with the devil.

When we're speaking in other tongues, we're talking to God, not the devil (Second Corinthians 14:2). The devil does not understand what I'm saying when I'm speaking in other tongues, for I'm speaking God-talk; it's a language that's between me and my Father.

We don't deal with the devil through speaking in other tongues; we deal with him through exercising our authority over him.

Through speaking in other tongues, my spirit was sensitive to the Spirit, and I perceived what the Spirit was revealing about the devil's plan to harm the child; but when the Spirit revealed that to me, then I dealt with the enemy using my authority.

About four months later, during one of our midweek services, I was telling the congregation about this incident when a young woman stood up. "Pastor, can I say something?" she called out.

"Yes, you can," I replied.

"I'm a member of a church about an hour away from

here, and I attend there on Sundays; but the drive there is too long for me to make during the week, so I attend here during the midweek service.

"I take care of my pastor's grandchildren; and I was with them a few weeks ago when all the staff was at the pastor's house for a Christmas party.

"The pastor's one-year old grandson got out of the house and was walking in the driveway behind a silver truck that belonged to a staff member. The staff member was leaving the party early, so he went out and got in his truck, but never saw the child behind him.

"He backed the truck up and ran over something. Not knowing what it was, he pulled forward over it again, intending to get out and see what he had hit. When he got out of the truck, he saw the one-year old boy lying in the driveway with tread marks across his abdomen and legs.

"Then the little boy jumped up, and ran in the house, showing everyone his tread marks – completely unharmed!"

So great is the power of God to keep and protect!

TRAGEDY AVERTED

On another occasion, I was praying in other tongues before going to sleep one night. As I laid there praying, I saw two vehicles collide, with one vehicle hitting the other one on the driver's side.

When I saw that, I said, "Satan, you take your hands off that situation. I bind the spirit of death; I loose the power of God and the angels of God to be around that situation."

I took a few minutes longer to pray in other tongues to make sure that there was nothing more I needed to do. I was clear in my spirit, so I fell off to sleep.

About two weeks later I received a phone call that let me know that there had been an accident involving an acquaintance of mine.

A drunk driver had hit this person on the driver's side so hard that the top of the car flew off. When the emergency team arrived on the scene, the car that had been hit was so mangled that the medical team pulled out the body bag; they didn't think there was any way the driver would survive an accident like that.

But after a time of cutting away the car to remove the driver, he had only minor injuries.

I believe in the power of God that delivers and rescues us from the enemy's plans!

A WOMAN ESCAPES

One night, as I lay in bed speaking in other tongues, I seemed to be standing in the small hallway of an older, worn house. The walls of the hallway were white, and the carpet was gold, and there were two doorways on the left that led to two other small rooms.

I walked past the first door and stood at the second door.

In that second room was a woman who had both of her hands and legs tied to a bed. I knew that she had been held captive for a long time, and was being repeatedly abused.

When I saw this, I spoke to the devil to take his hands off this situation, and told him to let the woman go free.

After that, I fell off to sleep, and didn't think much more about it.

Two days later, I had driven to a church about an hour from home to minister in their midweek service. As I was teaching on prayer that night, I felt impressed to tell what I had seen in prayer, and how I had dealt with it by the Spirit.

The next day, a woman who had been present in that service, called one of our staff members and asked, "Have you seen the news today? There's a story on all the news channels of a woman who had been kidnapped 20 years ago and has just escaped."

I knew that was the one I had been led of the Spirit to pray for.

When God can find those who will cooperate with the Spirit in prayer, He will be invited to move by His power in the lives of those who need His help. He is looking for opportunities to move in the lives of those who need Him, but He has to find someone to cooperate with Him. He is able to work more through those who will take the time to make their spirits sensitive to the Holy Spirit through speaking in other tongues.

I didn't have that experience in prayer because I'm a pastor; I had that experience because I take time to speak in other tongues.

There are many things that God would like to accomplish in our own lives, and in the lives of others, if we will just cooperate with the Spirit in prayer.

Speaking in other tongues is the door to the supernatural. The more we take time to speak in other tongues, which is a supernatural way of praying, the more the supernatural will flow in our lives.

As we speak in other tongues, we *build* a greater capacity for the supernatural to flow; for he that speaks in an unknown tongue builds himself.

PASTORING BY THE SPIRIT

As a pastor, I don't look to adopt what works for other pastors or churches, but I endeavor to pastor by the Spirit, looking to Him to lead and guide me; expecting Him to enlighten me with the methods that fit our congregation.

As I take time to speak in other tongues, the knowledge and leading of the Great Shepherd comes to my heart, and I receive light on how He wants our local church built. Any other method would fall short and miss the mark, and all the building would be in vain. *"Except the Lord build the house, they labour in vain that build it"* (Psalm 127:1).

PARENTING BY THE SPIRIT

As a mother, I've gone aside with the great Helper and spoken in other tongues to know His mind for our family and children. Through His guidance we have known who was and was not safe fellowship for our children. He helps us safeguard them from the fellowship that would pull them in the wrong direction.

As we took time to speak in other tongues, and took time to hear from Him, the training of our children has received the input and aid of our divine Helper.

He that speaks in an unknown tongue builds himself – his spirit, his life, his home, his family, his ministry, his purpose.

#3 – ORGANIZING BY THE SPIRIT

Let's look at the next definition Webster gave for the word "*edify*."

3) organize – He who speaks in an unknown tongue organizes himself.

Something that's organized carries an order with it. There is an order that hinders the Spirit from moving, but there is an order that caters to the moving of the Spirit. We are to carry the order in our life that caters to the moving of the Spirit.

We don't want so much order that the Spirit is pushed out, but we want the kind of order that builds a platform for the Spirit, and invites Him to move in our lives.

In a church service, our order can confine or limit what the Spirit is able to do, or we can create an order that gives Him total access and free rein to move among us.

The Pharisees had an order in their synagogues that forbade God to move or healings to occur on the Sabbath.

But on one occasion in particular, Jesus' order upset the Pharisees' order when He told a man with a withered hand to stretch it forth. As he did, it was made whole.

To the Pharisees, Jesus was intruding into and upsetting their order of things. But Jesus' order of following the Spirit of God set aside man's order, and it carried out God's plan to heal.

So, when we speak of the definition of "organize," we're referring to the kind of order that invites God's Spirit to move, and will interrupt man's lower order.

Sensitive to the Spirit in a Service

He that speaks in an unknown tongue will be sensitive to the order the Spirit wants to move in a church service, and he will allow the Spirit to have His way, responding to Him in a way that invites His movement.

Not only must the minister be sensitive, but the music leader must be sensitive, the ushers must be sensitive.

How does that come about? By speaking in other tongues, you make your own spirit sensitive to the order that the Holy Spirit wants to bring to a service.

Order in the Direction of a Ministry

For a ministry to carry proper order and organization, it must lay emphasis on what God wants that ministry to emphasize. We can't adopt what God told some other ministry to do, and expect to have proper order. We get out of divine order when we try to adopt for ourselves the direction God gave another man.

The needs of people and society are so vast, that to be effective you must have it clear in your own spirit what God wants your ministry to emphasize so that you don't get diverted by the vast amount of needs.

Don't allow family members, loved ones, staff, or congregation members to mingle their own vision and interests in with the divine order and organization God has for your ministry. Although they may have good ideas, that doesn't make them the plan of God, or the direction of God. God's order and directions to us must be guarded from well-meaning people.

ORDER IN THE FIVEFOLD OFFICES

A minister can even get out of order in the fivefold offices he may stand in.

Kenneth Hagin told of an incident in his own life that brings instruction to us. In the earlier years of his traveling ministry, Brother Hagin was leaving a church building after a service one night. As he stepped out of the building and onto the sidewalk, he slipped on the ice and landed on his elbow. He knew he had hurt his elbow, so the pastor of the church put him in his car and started driving him to the hospital. While on the way to the hospital, the Lord spoke to him and told him that he had not broken, but had fractured his elbow. Jesus told him not to worry about anything, and that He would speak to him about it later.

When Brother Hagin got to the hospital, the doctor confirmed what Jesus had already told him; nothing was broken, but there was a fracture.

They put Brother Hagin's arm in a sling, and had him to stay a few days in the hospital. One day, while in the hospital, Brother Hagin heard footsteps coming toward his hospital room. The door to his room opened and he assumed it was the nurse, but when he looked up, it was Jesus.

For an hour and a half Jesus talked to him about many things. But one of the things Jesus said to him was that it was not Him who had caused the accident; that the enemy had caused it. Yet, Jesus told him that although He didn't cause it, He did permit it.

Jesus went on to explain to Brother Hagin that in a church service two years before, he had announced to a congregation that he was called to be a teacher and a prophet. Jesus told him that when he announced that, Brother Hagin got out of his perfect will and moved into His permissive will. Jesus instructed Brother Hagin that he was called to be a prophet and a teacher, not a teacher and a prophet; he had gotten the offices reversed in their order.

Jesus explained to him that the prophet's office is a higher office than the teacher's office; therefore, by reversing the order of the two offices, he had put a lower office above the higher office. He told Brother Hagin that he was laying more emphasis on the lower office and operating more in that lower office than in the higher office as a prophet. By doing that, he would develop the teacher's office more than the prophet's office, and be out of God's will by doing that.

84

Jesus told Brother Hagin that he should be glad that He had permitted the accident to arrest his attention so that He could talk to him about the change he needed to make. If Brother Hagin would not have made that correction, then by being out of God's will, he would have opened the door to the enemy, and Satan would have been able to cause him to die prematurely, in his mid-50's. (This incident is recorded in Kenneth Hagin's book, *I Believe in Visions*).

Disobedience opens the door to the enemy; but when walking in God's perfect will, there's perfect protection. If accidents or tragedies are happening, find out from God where the open door to the enemy is, and get it closed.

God's people are redeemed from destruction, tragedy, crisis and accidents. So, if those things are happening, something's out of divine order. God will show you what needs to be corrected.

In relaying this incident to you, I want you to see how someone may get out of order in the fivefold offices he may stand in.

One definition of the word "edify" is to "organize". He that speaks in an unknown tongue edifies (organizes) himself (in the offices he may stand in).

Speaking in other tongues helps us to gain clarity in our spirits so that we can know the offices we may stand in, and helps us to keep them in proper order; thereby, staying in God's perfect will. The more you speak in other tongues, the clearer His plans and purposes for your life become.

ORDER IN DOCTRINES

Another thing that ministers must have in proper order is the doctrines they preach; and they must have the correct emphasis on those doctrines.

Many ministers have lost their anointing and ministries by majoring on things of minor importance. If the New Testament majors on it, then you can major on it. But if the New Testament lays minor importance on something, you are to lay minor importance on it. Major on the majors, and minor on the minors.

Many have gotten into ditches, even on major issues, and lost their ministries.

Many, ministers and believers alike, have become spiritually unsound by laying undue stress on things of minor importance.

Many ministries have been lost because they latched on to a wind of doctrine that was blowing around. The Word warns us against getting blown about by winds of doctrines; the Bible doesn't even call them winds of wrong doctrines, they're just doctrines that blow around that weren't to be majored on (Ephesians 4:14). We should let the winds of doctrine blow right on past us, and remain sure-footed on the balanced Word of God.

As ministers, we should feed the people sheep-food, which is the Word of God that helps them to live victorious in their everyday lives.

It's imperative to the longevity of a minister, and to the blessing of God's people, that any preaching that's done from the Old Testament be brought through Calvary.

86

Preach any Old Testament passages from the light given in the New Testament.

Jesus' death, burial, resurrection, ascension, and seating at the right hand of the Father sheds new light on Old Testament passages. Jesus' position at the right hand of the Father brought the church into a different position than the saints of the Old Testament had. Our preaching should be based on what belongs to the church now, based on what Jesus provided for us.

The doctrines we preach and hold to must bring faith, peace and blessing to God's people, not fear or division.

As we take time to speak in other tongues, we keep our spirits sensitive to the Holy Spirit, and we are more clearly able to know His teachings and instructions in the balance of the Word.

ORDER IN THE SPIRITUAL LIFE

When it comes to the spiritual health of the believer, there must be God's order in place to experience God's best.

Matthew 6:33 tells us,

But seek ye FIRST the kingdom of God, and His righteousness; and all these things (life's daily provisions) *shall be ADDED unto you.*

God's kingdom is a spiritual kingdom. It's not a business kingdom, nor a financial kingdom, but a spiritual kingdom. To seek first His kingdom is to put spiritual things first. Put your fellowship with God first. Put the development of your own spirit first. Put the local church first, for it's the only place in the earth that's dedicated to the feeding and education of the spirit of man. All other things come after spiritual things.

There are some Christians that will even take that to the extreme and get into a ditch, and not give proper attention to their family or to natural responsibilities that must be carried out. The scripture says, *"seek ye FIRST the kingdom of God."* It doesn't say, *"seek ye ONLY the kingdom of God."*

Keep priorities in their proper place. Don't let business, work, sports, or any other activities cause you to neglect your spiritual life, your church attendance, and your serving in the local church.

Parents need to keep their lives and the lives of their children purged from too many unimportant extracurricular activities and sports events. Sports and other activities are fine in their proper place. But to have your children involved in so many extra activities that you are only attending these extra events and playing full-time chauffeur, and spiritual things are being neglected, then things are out of order, and your life and family will eventually suffer the consequences.

If you're too busy to spend time in fellowship with God, and to be faithful to serve in your local church, you're too busy with the wrong things.

Spending time speaking in other tongues will help you keep your spirit sensitive to the order of the Spirit you should hold and protect in your daily spiritual life.

He that speaks in an unknown tongue edifies (organizes) himself.

#4 – ESTABLISHED IN THE SPIRITUAL ARENA

Let's see another definition Webster's dictionary gives for the word "edify."

4) establish – He that speaks in an unknown tongue establishes himself.

Establish means "to make firm, stable and fixed." To speak in other tongues will serve to stabilize the believer; it will help you to remain spiritually anchored – anchored in God's Word, anchored in God's blessings, anchored in fellowship with God, and not drifting away when the storms of adversity blow.

When winds of adversity, tests, and trials blow, you'll be fortified from within to stand your ground, kept from drifting into fear, doubt, and unbelief, not slipping into the mental arena, but keeping your mouth and thoughts hooked up to your heart.

For with stammering lips and another tongue will he speak to this people...This is the rest wherewith ye may cause the weary to rest; and this is the refreshing.

(Isaiah 28:11 & 12)

This passage is telling of the benefits of speaking in other tongues in the midst of adversity. The mind can be at peace, free from torment, and refreshing can come, even when faced with difficult circumstances.

To speak in other tongues is to establish and fix yourself on the spiritual arena instead of the natural arena and all its opposition. To speak in other tongues in the face of opposition is to help steady the gaze of your spiritual eyes, keep-

89

ing them fixed on the unseen and the eternal, and off of the trappings of the seen and temporal realm.

As one prays in other tongues, circumstances seem less formidable, the answer stays in view, and thoughts of failure can be laughed at, for you are established, stable and fixed in the spirit realm – the realm of victory.

Things that would pull others away from God's best, God's plan and God's blessings, won't find entrance into the one who keeps his spirit sensitive to God through speaking in other tongues.

Winds of doctrine (not necessarily wrong doctrines) will blow through the body of Christ, and these winds will cause some to lay undue emphasis on these dividing doctrines. But your spirit will be discerning and shored up against these things as you take time to speak in other tongues; you'll not drift away with them, rather, you'll be anchored, stable, fixed, and established in soundness.

Established in Your Local Church

Those who take time to speak much in other tongues won't be duped into being pulled away from their pastor and their local church. They will help establish themselves in their place in the local church family; they will be empowered to remain stable and fixed in the local church where God has placed them.

Matthew 9:35 & 36 shows us that those without a shepherd were sick, fainting (not finishing their spiritual race), and scattered (scattered health, scattered families, scattered finances). To be scattered spiritually is to be without an anointed man of God who speaks into your life and is a spiritual supply to you.

The enemy will seek to pull you away from your pastor, for then he would be able to cause you to faint and be scattered; but the believer who establishes himself through speaking in other tongues, will be sensitive to the Spirit of God, and will recognize the enemy's strategies. No offense will be received by the believer who stays full of the Spirit. No opportunity to abandon his pastor will be received.

He who speaks in an unknown tongue edifies (establishes, makes firm, and fixes) himself.

#5 – SPIRITUAL GROWTH

Let's see the next definition Webster gives for "edify."

5) grow – He that speaks in an unknown tongue grows himself. Speaking in other tongues plays a role in the process of spiritual growth and maturity.

Spiritual growth is much like physical growth. Physically speaking, every person is born as a baby; they grow to childhood, and then advance to full maturity.

The same thing is true spiritually speaking. When someone is born again, they are born as a babe in Christ, a spiritual baby. But as they feed on the Word, act on that Word, and develop their spirits, they will advance past spiritual childhood, and go on to spiritual maturity.

The defeat many believers experience in life is due to the fact that they never develop to full spiritual maturity, but remain spiritual babies; they don't take the time to feed on the Word, live full of the Spirit, and renew their minds with the Word through acting on the Word. Therefore, they think and act just like they did before they were even saved, and they give place to the devil in their life; they open the door to him.

The believer who takes time to speak in other tongues daily, fortifies himself from within, and tends to his spiritual growth; he makes steps toward the development of his own spirit.

BEARING MUCH FRUIT

Anyone who is growing spiritually will produce fruit; fruit is the evidence of that growth process.

We planted some fruit trees on our property that were very small and young. They came about waist high, but even though they were so small, there was still fully developed fruit on them. There weren't a lot of pieces of fruit, but the fruit that was there was fully developed. It was proof that the trees were healthy and growing.

If someone's spiritual life is growing and developing, there will be fruit in their life; there will be fruit if the Word is operating in their spirits.

Even newborn babes in Christ will bear a measure of fruit. Like those baby fruit trees we planted, they may not have a great measure of fruit, but there will be fruit that's apparent and a blessing to others.

Jesus tells us that you'll know people's lives by their fruit. It's not up to God to develop your spiritual life – it's up to you. One means He has given us to help us develop spiritually is through the privilege of speaking in other tongues.

Anyone who walks by those fruit trees in our yard can see the fruit.

Likewise, when you take time to speak in other tongues, others will be able to see the fruit of that.

On the other hand, when believers neglect the privilege of speaking in other tongues, the barrenness of fruit will also be obvious to those around them.

John 15:8 tells us that Jesus stated, *"Herein is My Father glorified, that ye bear MUCH FRUIT."* The greater the measure of fruit in a believer's life, the more God is glorified. God doesn't receive the greatest glory when His children remain spiritual babies, but He does when we go on to full spiritual maturity. Through speaking in other tongues, that maturing process is aided.

He that speaks in an unknown tongue edifies (grows or develops) himself.

#6 – PROSPERITY

Let's see the next definition given by Webster for the word "edify."

6) prosper – He who speaks in unknown tongues prospers himself.

When you speak in an unknown tongue, you are speaking to God (First Corinthians 14:2), the God of all wisdom, knowledge, and understanding. When you speak in other tongues, you are fellowshipping with all wisdom, knowledge, and understanding. In God's wisdom is the ability for you to live a prosperous life.

"I'LL MAKE YOU RICH!"

On one occasion, Jesus appeared to Kenneth Hagin in a vision. In the course of His conversation with him, Jesus stated, "If you'll learn to follow My Spirit, I'll make you rich. I'm not opposed to my people being rich; I'm opposed to them being covetous."

To be rich means to have a full supply and lacking nothing.

Jesus wasn't telling Brother Hagin that He was going to make all His children millionaires, but He was saying that if they will learn to follow the Spirit of God, they will have a full supply, and they won't lack for anything; they will have enough for themselves, and still be able to give to others.

But notice that what Jesus said made it conditional, *"If* you'll learn to follow My Spirit."

We stated earlier that the primary way you make your own spirit sensitive to the voice of the Holy Spirit is through speaking in other tongues.

Psalm 1:3 tells us about the one who meditates in the Word, *"whatsoever he doeth shall prosper."* But you need to follow the Spirit's guidance on what you should set your hand to. Don't just randomly decide what you should labor in or be employed in; let the Spirit guide you in the business affairs of life. When the Spirit leads you to set your hand to a particular thing, then you know that it will prosper because you're following the Spirit; and He always leads you into success, but never into failure. If we fail in some area, it's only because we failed to fully follow Him.

Through speaking in other tongues, your spirit will gain clarity of what the Holy Spirit is leading you to set your hand to.

Too many times, believers don't take time to get clarity in their own spirit of how the Spirit of God is leading them before they make financial or business moves, and they end up creating great difficulties for themselves and their families.

But as we take time to feed and meditate on the Word, and to speak in other tongues, we set ourselves up for financial success. The Spirit of God will make you successful in business.

You're not limited to your own education and knowledge, but you have access to His great wisdom. When you follow the wisdom He gives, God will make you brilliant by the Holy Ghost.

Men will be astounded at your success and ability, as you access God's wisdom and ability through speaking in other tongues. To speak in other tongues is to fellowship with the wisdom of the One who founded all creation.

ACCESS THE GREATER ONE

One minister from another country walked through a popular amusement park in the United States, and as he did, tears streamed down his face. Other minister friends walking with him asked, "Is something wrong?"

"No," he answered. "I was just thinking that if a man who didn't know God could build all of this, how much more should Christians, who have God's own Spirit living in them, be able to accomplish!"

We have not fully accessed all that is made available to us as God's own children. We have set aside fellowship with God in preference for fellowship with man. We have neglected the mighty privileges of feeding on God's Word and speaking in other tongues; then we wonder why things don't work for us as they should.

Let's take our rightful place at the table of His Word and feed our spirits with life.

Let's yield to the help of the greater One on the inside as He gives us utterances to speak in other tongues.

Let's co-labor with God and accomplish all that He intended, using His mighty wisdom and ability.

Let's lay aside weights and hindrances that hold us back and run as He intended; run with clarity, run with accuracy, run in His ability, and carry out His plan and purpose for our lives.

Living full of the Word and the Spirit is the only way to accomplish living in its highest sense; it's the only way to really live.

DIVINE IDEAS

One single mom gave the testimony of being in a service where the Spirit of God spoke to her to give the minister $1000 toward his ministry. She didn't have $1000 at the time, but she knew God spoke to her to give it, so she wrote a pledge on an offering envelope, committing to pay the $1000 within 30 days.

When she got back home, she told the Lord that she did not have the money to pay the pledge, but that she trusted Him to cause the money to come to her.

As she was talking to the Lord about it, He reminded her of decorative barrettes she had made at Christmas time to give to some of her friends and relatives. The Lord prompted her to make more of those and sell them.

So, she made up many of the barrettes, and asked a friend, who owned a clothing boutique, if she could set up a table to sell the barrettes in her shop. The friend welcomed her to sell them in her shop. So, she set up a table, laid them all out, and waited for interested customers to come.

After a little while, a woman came into the boutique and walked up to the table. One by one she picked up the barrettes and studied them.

"Did you make these?" the woman inquired.

"Yes, I did," the single mom replied.

"I'll take 50,000 of them!" The woman was a buyer for a major nationwide department store.

Not only did the single mom now have money to pay her pledge, but now she had a new source of income. God gave her a divine idea, and it changed her financial setting.

When you take time to speak in other tongues, you start tapping into mysteries beyond your own understanding (Second Corinthians 14:2). In those mysteries are divine ideas for your financial increase. God will give you divine ideas for your business, your department, and your position. You'll profit from speaking in other tongues.

If finances are running low, don't assume that working more hours or getting a second job is your solution. Take time to feed on God's Word and to speak in other tongues. As you do, you'll tap into God's wisdom for your financial prosperity.

One minister stated, "The greatest financial breakthroughs came for my ministry after long seasons of speaking in other tongues."

By speaking in other tongues, we access God's wisdom and mysteries, and we gain His understanding of what steps we may need to take to enjoy the fullness of His supply for our financial welfare.

He who speaks in an unknown tongue edifies (prospers) himself.

#7 – SPIRITUAL PROSPERITY

Let's see the last definition Webster gave for the word "edify."

7) to profit spiritually – He who speaks in an unknown tongue profits spiritually.

If there's profit, there's increase. The direction of God is increase. The movement of God is increase. Every step He leads us in is toward our own increase. Sometimes, the natural may look like we're decreasing, but it will end up in our increase.

When God told us to move our ministry from Oklahoma to California, it looked like we were decreasing in finances, in land, and in other things. But as we stayed faithful, the increase surpassed the decrease of those things, and we ended up having more in California than we ever did in Oklahoma.

Full provision is in the place where God told you to be. It may not look like increase for a time, but if you'll stay faithful to God's plan for your life, you'll see that the direction and movement of God is always toward your increase.

To profit spiritually, we must be walking out God's plan for our lives; and one primary way you gain clarity of God's plan for your life and ministry is through speaking in other tongues.

The more you speak in other tongues, the more His plan unfolds to you. The more you take time to speak to God in other tongues, the greater clarity you gain in your own spirit of His plan for you. Then, the more fully you walk out His plan and purpose for you, the more He will be able to increase the measure of anointing on your life and ministry.

To "profit spiritually" would mean to increase in the anointing, to increase in the fruit of your life and ministry, to increase in the revelation of God's Word, to increase in your ability to discern the leading of the Holy Spirit, and a host of other blessings.

The spiritual profit we gain from speaking in other tongues is measureless; there's no limit to what can be gained as we take time to fellowship with the Father through speaking in other tongues.

CHAPTER EIGHT

Other Benefits of Speaking in Tongues

"*But ye, beloved, building up yourselves on your most holy faith, praying in the Holy Ghost* (in other tongues)" (Jude 20). Speaking in other tongues assists your faith.

What does it do for faith? It builds up the faith you possess – it strengthens it.

Faith *comes* by hearing, and hearing by the Word of God (Romans 10:17), but faith doesn't *operate* by hearing. Faith is *released* and *operates* through speaking words of faith, and through actions of faith.

Faith doesn't come by speaking in other tongues, for the Word tells us that faith comes by hearing the Word, but the faith we have is built up and strengthened by speaking in other tongues.

Faith is resident in the spirit of every believer, for Romans 12:3 tells us that God has given to each of His children the measure of faith. When we were born again, God gave us all the same measure of faith. However, the Word teaches us that the measure of faith can be increased or diminished.

We want to increase our measure of faith, but we also want to strengthen the faith we already possess.

If you were to see a body builder, you may say, "They've got more muscles than I do." But really, they don't. They have the exact same number of muscles as you do; they just built up and strengthened the muscles they do have.

That's what speaking in tongues does for your faith muscle; it doesn't give you more faith, but it does build up and strengthen the faith you have, making it easier to lift things with your faith.

Many Christians fail because they try to spend faith before they've taken the time to strengthen that faith. Faith comes through hearing the Word, but for faith to be the most productive and accomplish the most for you, it must be strengthened, and that's done through speaking in other tongues.

If there was a 300 pound item in the middle of my floor that needed moving, I could struggle with it myself and make very little progress in moving it, or I could get several people together to help me move it, or I could get a strong muscle builder to move it.

Likewise, many believers fail to move difficulties out of their lives because they have weak faith; they haven't taken the time to strengthen it before they use it, so they make very little progress in getting that difficulty moved. So, they end up relying on trying to get others to add their faith to the need. But it's best to become a spiritual strong man by building up your own faith so that you have the strength to overcome that difficulty with your own faith.

Faith is built up through exercising it through use, but it's also built up through speaking in tongues.

If you're faced with a test or trial that you've made very little progress against, feed your faith on the Word, build up that faith through speaking in other tongues, and then use your faith. As you take these steps, you'll find that faith won't be a struggle, but it will flow easily for you.

You are to be a superman in faith. If that's to be accomplished, however, don't leave out the vital step of building up the faith you possess through speaking in other tongues.

WALKING IN LOVE

We know that the Word tells us that faith works by love (Galatians 5:6).

Love is to faith what gasoline is to a car. Just as a car won't go anywhere unless there's gasoline in it, faith won't go anywhere unless love is fueling it. When love stops flowing, faith won't go anywhere.

Jude 20 & 21 also gives us instruction in this.

> *But ye, beloved, building up yourselves on your most holy faith, PRAYING IN THE HOLY GHOST, KEEP YOURSELVES IN THE LOVE OF GOD.*

By taking time to speak in other tongues, you not only build up the faith you possess, but you hold yourself in the place of walking in love.

When you're confronted with an unlovely situation, instead of jumping right in with your mouth, take time to go aside and speak in other tongues. It will keep your flesh under the dominion of your spirit. If you talk out of the feelings and emotions of your flesh, you may say something that you shouldn't say; but if you talk out of your heart, the love of God is in your heart, so love will reply instead of offense.

MORTIFYING THE DEEDS OF THE FLESH

Romans 8:13 tells us that we mortify (deaden) the deeds of the flesh through the Spirit.

Every man has things present in their flesh that will trip them up, and cause them to miss the mark if those things go unchecked.

Hebrews 12:1 instructs us to,

...let us lay aside every weight (the things that slow down our progress), and the sin which doth so easily beset us...

"If the Son therefore shall make you free, ye shall be free indeed" (John 8:36). Jesus has paid the price to free us from those things that weaken us and open us up to defeat. We are to walk free from those things, and we have the Holy Spirit to help us mortify the deeds of the flesh that trouble us.

HABITS GOVERN US

A man's life is a picture of his habits.

God gave us habit-forming ability so that we could form the right habits to help shape our lives.

Jesus had the spiritual habit of rising early to go to an alone place to pray. He didn't make it a law, for that would have brought bondage; but He made it a habit to govern His life. In Luke 22:39, The Amplified Bible reads, *"And He came out and went, as was His habit, to the Mount of Olives."*

Jesus also had the spiritual habit of faithful church attendance, for Luke 4:16 tells us, *"as his custom* (habit) *was, he went into the synagogue on the Sabbath day."*

With this habit-forming ability, we are to establish good spiritual habits, as well as good mental and physical habits that will bless and shape our lives.

However, before we were born again, we sometimes established bad habits instead of good habits, then those habits we had formed were points of weakness for us once we got born again.

But we're not left to ourselves to overcome those bad habits in our own human ability; we have the Holy Spirit to help us. We're not left to just rely upon human willpower and self-help methods to overcome these bad habits.

We're not left to our own human ability to establish good habits either; we have the help of the Holy Spirit available to us.

As Romans 8:13 tells us, we *"through the Spirit do mortify the deeds of the body."* We can employ our great Helper, the Holy Spirit, to aid us in rising above these weaknesses, and replace them with good habits to help shape our spiritual, mental and physical lives. We are fortified from within as we take time to pray in other tongues; for praying in tongues is a spiritual action that helps our spirits to dominate over the mental and the physical arenas, where many bad habits exist. Speaking in other tongues makes us more spirit-conscious; thereby, the mental and the physical arenas lose sway over us.

Worry is a bad mental habit. Complaining and grumbling are bad mental habits. Being critical is a bad habit that must be changed.

Smoking, drinking, drugs, and overeating are all bad physical habits that must be changed; but we have help in doing it! We have the great Helper!

He will strengthen and fortify us from within as we feed on the Word of God, and as we take time to speak in other tongues.

If you will implement these good spiritual habits of feeding on the Word and edifying yourself through speaking in other tongues on a daily basis, you will be assisted in overcoming bad habits and implementing other good habits in your life.

Don't focus on getting the bad habit out. Focus on implementing good habits. The good habits will displace the bad ones.

One of the rising problems in Americans is that of overeating; but we have help to fortify us against this bad habit. If we will feed on the Word, and take time to speak in other tongues, especially before meals, we will be fortified from within to resist that bad habit. We're not simply left to willpower and self-help methods. We can mortify (deaden) the deeds of the flesh through the Spirit.

CHAPTER NINE

"Let Him Pray"

"Is any among you afflicted? let him pray" (James 5:13). The Greek (the New Testament was originally written in Greek) actually states that the word "afflicted" in this verse means, "going through a test or trial." So, we could read the verse this way, "Is any among you going through a test or trial? Let him pray."

Notice who's supposed to do the praying – the one who's going through the test or trial. It doesn't say that if you're going through a test or trial to get a counseling appointment; it says to *"let him pray."* To go to the pastor for counseling when you haven't yet prayed is to get off the Word.

The rest of James 5:13 reads, *"Is any merry? let him sing psalms."*

If a Christian walked up to you and said with a sad, long face, "God just provided the money I need to pay my mortgage. I'm so happy. Would you sing for me?" It would sound laughable, wouldn't it? If you're happy, you do your own singing.

James is trying to show us that as absurd as it would be for you to ask someone to do your singing for you because you're happy, it would be just as absurd to ask someone else to do your praying for you because you're going through a test or trial.

If I'm happy, I'll do my own singing.

If I'm going through a test or trial, I'll do my own praying. No one can pray about what I'm going through like I can, because the situation is closer to me than it is to anyone else.

Now, you may ask someone to agree with you in prayer, but we never ask someone to pray for us just so we can be dismissed from the responsibility of praying for ourselves.

DO SOMETHING SPIRITUAL

When test or trials come in life, the tendency of some Christians is to do something in the natural to deal with it, because they live their lives strictly in the natural.

But James is instructing us, when we're faced with a test and trial to do something supernatural; do something spiritual – pray! Don't revert back to the natural when faced with a test and trial; but stay in the spirit. Do something supernatural – pray!

How's the best way to pray when going through a test or trial? In the spirit, in other tongues; for Second Corinthians 14:2 tells us that when we speak in other tongues, we're speaking divine secrets and mysteries with God.

Tell God that you're lifting up this test before Him so that you can receive His help and guidance on it, and then look to the Holy Spirit to give you utterance in talking to God about it more fully.

As you are speaking in other tongues about your situation, quiet your mind and focus on your spirit. Don't focus on the test, but rather, focus on your spirit.

God may enlighten you with a certain scripture. He may give you instructions. He may quicken you to read a certain passage in your Bible. But as you quiet your mind and focus on your spirit, His guidance and instruction will float up from your spirit and enlighten your mind.

It may take a few times of waiting before the Lord like this before enlightenment comes. It's not that God is slow to speak; rather, we are sometimes slow to hear because we've been too busy with natural things, or we are having difficulty quieting our minds.

As we take the time to wait before Him, He will give perfect guidance.

CHAPTER TEN

Making Power Available

James 5:16 (The Amplified Bible), tells us,

The earnest (heartfelt, continued) prayer of a righteous man makes tremendous power available [dynamic in its working].

The word *"earnest"* and *"heartfelt"* are very descriptive words, but they aren't describing a natural, human feeling or emotion. It's not talking about appearing to be earnest and heartfelt physically when you pray, by walking the floor, or by making movements or motions with the body; but it's talking about an earnest and heartfelt condition of your spirit toward a particular person or situation you're praying about.

I've laid in bed at night and prayed quietly about something which my spirit was earnest and heartfelt about, but never lifted my voice above a whisper.

Now, don't misunderstand me. There may be times that your spirit gets so moved upon by the spirit of prayer that you get louder when you pray. But you aren't to try to manufacture something physically to make you appear to be earnest or heartfelt when you pray.

When the Spirit of God moves upon you to pray about something, He is earnest and heartfelt about getting help to that situation. You will sense His earnestness toward it, and your spirit picks up on the urgency and earnestness the Spirit has toward the situation; and you are to continue to lift up that situation to God in prayer until you have laid hold of the answer.

PRAYING FOR OTHER PEOPLE

Your prayer life is not to change the will of other people, or to try to get God to change the will of other people. God won't violate a man's will, and the prayer to change a man's will goes unanswered. God gave man the ability to make his own choices, and God won't go against what a man chooses for himself. We can't make choices for other people, and God won't make choices for other people; they must make choices for themselves.

Prayer is not designed to force things on people; that's how the devil operates, but not God.

However, James does tell us what our prayers will accomplish on the behalf of others. It will make *"tremendous power available"* to them. When God's power is made available to others, it makes it easier for them to make the right choices.

THE POWER IS PRESENT

Jesus appeared to Kenneth Hagin on one occasion and told him, "The power of God is present everywhere. There is enough power in every sick room and in every hospital room to raise up that sick one if they only knew it was present, and would give it action."

He went on to say, "When I was on the earth, I was the power of God. If people needed the power of God, they had to get to where I was to receive that power. But now, the Holy Ghost is the power of God. The Holy Ghost came to reside on the earth on the Day of Pentecost, and He's present everywhere, so power is present everywhere.

"If people only knew that power was present, and would give it action, that power would raise up that sick one."

It's not enough for God's power to be present, someone has to have faith in that power, and give action to that power.

In Second Corinthians 2:5 Paul says,

That your faith should not stand in the wisdom of men, but (that your faith should stand) in the power of God.

We must believe in that power, and we must speak words to release the power of God to flow.

God's power is present in your house, your car, your workplace, anywhere you may go; His power is present everywhere because the Holy Ghost is present everywhere. If you need something from God, you don't have to wait till you get to church to have the pastor to pray for you. You can receive whatever you need from that power that is present.

God has put His power at your disposal to use as it is needed. You don't have to wait for God to initiate the movement of His power. You don't have to wait for Him to send power your direction. His power is present everywhere so that you will have it at your disposal as needed.

Smith Wigglesworth would upset religious people with a statement he often made in his services. He stated, "If the Spirit of God doesn't move me, I move Him!" Religion got offended at him, thinking that he would dare presume to move the Spirit.

But Brother Wigglesworth understood that all power and ability was available to him to use as it was needed.

Jesus declared,

> *Behold, I GIVE UNTO YOU POWER to tread on serpents and scorpions, and over all the power of the enemy: and nothing shall by any means hurt you.*
> (Luke 10:19)

We have the power available to use any time we are faced with anything that is of the enemy.

We don't have to wait for God to initiate power in our direction. His power is present, and we can activate that power with our faith whenever it's needed; and it will move wherever people will cooperate with it.

Smith Wigglesworth knew that there may be times that God will initiate some things, but if He doesn't, the Holy Spirit is ever present, so power is ever present. We can activate that power and cooperate with that power as we exercise faith in that power.

CAUSING THE POWER TO FLOW

Just because the power of God is present everywhere doesn't mean that it's moving or flowing. You have to release faith for the power of God that is present to flow. Jesus told Brother Hagin that the power was present everywhere, but that someone had to give it action. Someone had to activate it with their faith.

In California a lot of the kids have piñatas at their birthday parties. (A piñata is a cardboard animal or figure that's filled with candy and small treats.) The piñata is hung from a high place, and children are blindfolded one at a time, and given a chance to swing at the piñata with a stick. If they hit the piñata just right, it will break open and all the kids will gather up the candy and treats. All the kids get to collect the candy and treats, even if they aren't the one who broke open the piñata.

Likewise, the power of God is present everywhere, but like that piñata, none of what that power contains will flow until someone strikes it. But once someone strikes the power with their faith and causes it to flow, everyone is free to gather up the benefits of that power, even if they aren't the ones who struck it.

How do you strike the power of God?

Your words of faith are like the stick that strikes the piñata, causing the power to flow. You are to say, "I believe the power of God is present; therefore, I speak for that power to flow into my body. I speak for that power to flow into my finances."

You don't have to wait for God to move in those arenas of your life. He has put His power at your disposal, and given you the freedom to assign it to work any time and anywhere you need it to.

115

He has put His power at the disposal of all His children to use any time they will.

You must believe that the power is present. You must then speak words of faith that assign that power, telling that power where to flow. Tell it to flow into your body, into your finances, into your marriage, etc.

A LANDING PAD FOR GOD'S POWER

When we go to land our airplane, we can't land just anywhere. We can't land in a field or on a highway; we have to land in a place that's prepared for the airplane – on a runway.

Likewise, God's power can't land just anywhere. It can only land where faith has prepared a place for it. With words of faith we have to lay a runway, a landing pad for the power of God. We have to assign it a place to land.

God's power doesn't just move randomly. It moves where faith has prepared a place for it. By speaking for the power of God to move into your body, your finances, your business, etc., you are assigning it a place and preparing a landing pad for it.

OTHERS MUST RECEIVE THE POWER OF GOD

When we pray for someone else, we can make that same power available to them for their needs.

Notice what James 5:16 tells us regarding our prayer life,

116

The earnest (heartfelt, continued) prayer of a right-eous man MAKES TREMENDOUS POWER AVAILABLE [dynamic in its working].

(The Amplified Bible)

Our prayer life is not to change the wills of other people, but we can make this mighty power *available* to them; we can give it action toward their life.

Remember, power is present everywhere, but just because it's present doesn't mean it's flowing, or available. It takes someone with faith to strike the power of God with their words to make it flow, to make it available.

You may be praying for someone who doesn't know about God's power; they don't know that it's present where they are, and they don't know how to make it flow. But God will allow you to exercise faith on their behalf, and get the power flowing so that they can receive the help they need from that power. Your faith can make God's power available to them.

But, they still have a part to play! They must *receive* the power. You can make the power available to them, but you can't receive it for them. Receiving the power is an act of their own will that they must do, or it won't work for them.

We can pray before a church service and exercise faith for God's healing power to flow to the sick that will be in the service. Hands can be laid on the sick people who are present, but they still are the ones who have to cooperate with that power that's made available to them, and they must receive it into their bodies. If they resist it, it won't work for them, even though it was available to them.

STOCKING THE SHELVES

One day, we arrived back in town after flying in from a church service at 1:30 in the morning. Driving home from the airport, we passed a store, and my nine year old son said, "Let's go shopping in that store."

I said, "No, they're closed. It's the middle of the night."

"No," he exclaimed, "it's open. There are a lot of cars in the parking lot."

"Those are workers who are stocking the shelves. They're putting all the items out on the shelves to make things available for tomorrow's customers," I explained.

When I go shopping at that store, there are thousands of items that are available to me, but I only select the ones I want.

When we pray for others, we are doing the same thing those workers in the store were doing – we are stocking the shelves around people's lives, making power available to them.

Although we stock the shelves, making power available to them, they must still receive that power for themselves; we can't make them take it. But we can so fully stock the shelves around their lives that it makes it easy for them to reach out and take what they need. We can stock the power of God around them so richly that every time they make a move, they bump into that power, making it easy for them to receive of it. The more power we stock around them, the easier it is for them to make the right choices.

We want to do as James 5:16 says and make a "tremendous" measure of power available to them, not just a minimal measure, but a tremendous measure. The more faith we release in their behalf, the more power we stock around their life, and the easier it is for them to make the right choices.

CONTINUE TO RELEASE FAITH

How do we make a tremendous measure of power available to someone? We continue to lift them up before God.

Everyday we say, "Father, I believe in the power of God that's present around that brother, and I believe that it's flowing into his life now, and I thank You for it, in Jesus' Name." The more we release faith in the power by speaking words like that, the greater the measure of power that is made available to them.

"TELL HER THAT HER FAITH WORKED!"

A minister called me one day and asked for some input regarding one of the ladies in his congregation. The woman had been divorced for 20 years from a man who had never been born again, and declared that he didn't want to be born again.

For the past 20 years this ex-wife had been praying, believing in God to restore their marriage.

This minister had counseled with the woman to go on with her life and to quit waiting for her ex-husband to return; but she wouldn't. She said that if he didn't return that it would mean that her faith failed.

"What would you say to this woman to help her to see that she needs to move on with her life?" the minister asked.

I told this minister, "You tell the woman that her faith worked!"

"What do you mean?" he asked.

I told him, "James 5:16 said that when we pray for others, we make a tremendous measure of power available to them. If she's been praying in faith for him for 20 years, he has had a tremendous measure of power made available to him, but he has declined it! He chose not to receive it!

"Her faith can't receive the power for him. Her faith will only make the power available to him to receive. Her faith caused the power to flow in his direction, but he's been rejecting it for 20 years. You tell her that her faith worked! It made God's power available to him, but he didn't want it. God didn't fail! Her faith didn't fail! The man is the one who failed!"

We have to understand what the Word tells us that our prayer life will accomplish on the behalf of others. If they don't receive the power, don't question or doubt God's Word. Don't doubt your prayer life. Doubt the one who declined the power.

The Word works! Faith works! The prayers of a righteous man work! Praying in line with God's Word works!

But people don't receive the power if they fail to respond to it or cooperate with it.

Don't doubt the effectiveness of the Word. Don't doubt your faith or your prayer life. You faith is only intended to make power available to others, but you can't receive it or respond to that power for them – they have to do that.

POWER TO RAISE A DYING MAN

Dr. Lester Sumrall's testimony of healing tells how he benefited from God's power made available to him. As a 17-year old, he came down with tuberculosis and was given up to die.

His mother was a praying woman, and often brought her prayer group in his sick room to pray for him. But since he had run from God all his life, he would just pull the covers up over his head while they prayed.

One day the doctor gave his family the bad news that the young man wouldn't live through the night. He signed his death certificate, and then told his daddy to go buy him a burial plot.

But as the young Lester Sumrall lay dying that night, a coffin appeared on one side of his bed; it was tilted toward him, ready for him to be rolled into it.

As he rolled over in the bed, turning his back on that awful vision of the coffin, on the other side of the bed there was a giant Bible from the floor to the ceiling.

Then, God said, "Tonight you choose! You either preach My Word, or they will roll you into that coffin!"

The choice was an easy one. He said yes to God, and yes to His Word.

Instantly, he was raised up, completely whole.

Dr. Lester Sumrall went on to become one of the mightiest apostles of our day. Some would say that God spared his life through that deathbed experience because he was called to preach. But that's not the case.

He had that experience, and had his life spared because his mother prayed and made a tremendous measure of power available to him.

That power manifested to him in the form of a vision and in healing power.

That vision made his choice easy. The power made available to him made his choice easy. Although his mother's prayers of faith made a tremendous measure of power available to the young Lester Sumrall, he still had to make the choice to receive that power and to cooperate with it. He still had to say yes to God.

We don't pray for God to give visions to people, because we don't have a scriptural basis on which to base that kind of a prayer. The Word doesn't tell us that we can have faith to see visions or to claim them. Those things only happen as the Spirit wills.

But we can be assured that when we pray for others, a tremendous measure of God's power is made available to them, and God will employ whatever means necessary to make it easy for them to make the right choice.

CHAPTER ELEVEN

Continuing in Prayer

On one occasion years ago, as I would pray, I would sense that God was endeavoring to get something over to me, but I knew I was missing that; I wasn't receiving that into my spirit. So, I took some time aside to do some extra praying.

As I did, I said to God, "It seems to me that You've been endeavoring to get something over to me, but somehow I have failed to receive that into my spirit. If I'm right, I ask you to give that to me now."

God spoke back, "You're right. I have been endeavoring to get something over to you. You're missing it in your prayer life. You make requests of Me, but then you just let them drop. You need to continue in prayer.

"Remember the autobiography of George Mueller. Remember his accounts of how he prayed. He continued in prayer until his request was fulfilled. You need to continue in prayer."

(George Mueller was a minister in England who lived in the 1800's, and housed thousands of orphans in his orphanages.)

I did remember the accounts of how George Mueller prayed. In his prayer journal, he noted the number of times he would lift a particular need up before the Lord. He would bring the same need before God hundreds and hundreds of times until he saw its fulfillment. He didn't ask God for the same thing over and over, but he would thank God daily for supplying the answers to the requests he had made; and he did that everyday until he saw their fulfillment.

James 5:16 states,

> *The earnest, (heartfelt, CONTINUED) prayer of a righteous man makes tremendous power available [dynamic in its working].*

I knew that when God said that I needed to continue in prayer, that He wasn't telling me to ask for the same thing over and over again.

God reminded me of the scripture in Colossians 4:2, which states, *"Continue in prayer, and watch in the same with thanksgiving."* This verse tells us to continue in prayer, but it also tells us how to continue, or what it means to continue in prayer. We are to *"watch in the same* (watch over that request we made) *with thanksgiving."*

Too many times, we just think that praying means making requests of God; but there are many different kinds of prayer. There is the *prayer of supplication*, where we make requests of God. But there is also the *prayer of praise and worship*, where we give thanks to God.

When we're told in Colossians 4:2 to *"Continue in prayer,"* it's not telling us to continue with the same kind of prayer.

We are to pray the *prayer of supplication* when we make a request of God; but after we make the request, we don't continue asking for that same situation over and over. From then on we are to enter into thanksgiving with the *prayer of praise and worship*, thanking God for hearing us when we made the request, and for causing the answer and supply to come to us.

That's what Colossians 4:2 tells us to do, *"Continue in prayer, and watch in the same* (watch over that request we made) *with thanksgiving."*

God taught me that day that once I request something, or release my faith for something, from then on to thank Him daily for the fulfillment of that.

You don't have to make some long prayer in thanking Him. You can simply say, "Thank You, Father, that I have the answer to that situation."

When you do thank Him, release faith with those words. Let those words come from your heart, not just your head, but from your heart.

Ephesians 1:16 records that Paul said, *"Cease not to give thanks for you, making MENTION of you in my prayers."* He didn't make some long prayer in their behalf; he just made mention of them. A mention is enough if faith is released at the mention.

As we stated earlier, power only flows when faith is released. Your words of faith assign the power. Those words create a landing pad for the power of God.

The reason we must continue in prayer through giving God thanks, is that as we do, we continue to release our faith toward that situation; and the power continues to flow only as long as our faith continues to be released.

If faith stops flowing, power stops flowing. If faith continues to flow, power continues to flow. We continue in thanksgiving so that our faith will continue toward that situation; thereby, God's power will continue to flow toward that situation.

We are to believe that at the time we made our requests before God, that things started changing. We are to believe that power started flowing toward that situation at the time we first make the request.

But we must also continue to fuel that power toward our situation through the giving of thanks until we see its fulfillment.

When you first release your faith in prayer, the power to bring the answer starts moving in your life, but if that power is to continue moving toward your situation, faith has to continue to flow.

Thanksgiving is the voice of faith; faith flows as we give thanks to God. As we continue to give thanks to God in faith, power continues to flow.

Jesus stated, *"blessed are they that have not seen, and yet have believed"* (John 20:29). It honors God when we give Him thanks before we have any physical evidence of being heard.

We must not only make requests of God, but we must continue with the voice of thanksgiving until we see its fulfillment.

Let's not just wander around in prayer with no real direction or purpose. But let's be very definite about what we are coming before the Lord to obtain, and let's continue with purpose until we see that request fulfilled.

CHAPTER TWELVE

The Spirit of Prayer

Hebrews 4:15-16 tells us,

> *For we have not a high priest which cannot be TOUCHED WITH THE FEELING OF OUR INFIRMITIES; but was in all points tempted like as we are, yet without sin. Let us therefore come boldly unto the throne of grace, that we may obtain mercy, and find grace to help in time of need.*

Jesus feels what another feels; and as we enter into this great privilege of prayer, cooperating with the Spirit of God, we too will feel what Jesus feels for another. We will feel the agony of the Holy Spirit reaching out to God through us on their behalf.

When we sense in our spirits this great longing of the Spirit through us on the behalf of another, we know what we are to do. We are to *"come boldly unto the throne of grace that we may OBTAIN."* We are to come before the throne on the behalf of those who don't know how to access the throne for themselves. The throne is the place of obtaining. No need goes unmet at the throne.

How are we to come before the throne? We are to lift others up in the Spirit, praying for them in other tongues as the Holy Spirit moves upon us in love and compassion toward them.

FIRST EXPERIENCES

As I began to grow and develop spiritually over the years, so did my prayer life.

I began to have some experiences that I didn't understand. These experiences involved the spirit of prayer coming on me; but because I was untaught in these areas, I didn't always fully cooperate with the Holy Spirit, or even know what was happening.

However, over the past years, the Holy Spirit has been faithful to instruct and guide me into more understanding of these matters.

I share some of these experiences with you in the hopes of clarifying and defining for you some of these things that you too may have experienced, and yet not recognized as the spirit of prayer.

Because I didn't understand some of the things I was experiencing, at times, I was greatly troubled by them. Therefore, I hope that in the telling of them, you will avoid some of the struggles I faced in learning these things.

I first started having some of these stronger experiences in prayer soon after my husband and I were married.

We would make some trips overseas to minister, and as we would arrive, I would have an overwhelming sense of depression, sadness, and grieving come on me.

As I had only been born again and filled with the Holy Spirit for just a short time, I became greatly troubled by this, having no idea that this great sense of depression and grieving was the spirit of prayer moving upon me.

THE ENEMY'S STRATEGIES

The devil took advantage of my lack of knowledge in these things and bombarded me with thoughts that suggested something was wrong with me.

The greatest weapon our enemy uses is the power of suggestion. He suggests a thought to us, and if we don't recognize it as from him and stand against it, he will gain entrance into our thought life, and we will yield up our peace.

The enemy was seeking to hold me in the mental arena because that's the arena he deals in; that's his arena.

If Satan can hold you in the mental arena, he'll whip you; but if you'll hold him in the arena of the spirit, which is the arena of faith, you'll whip him.

He seeks to hold us in the mental arena, for then we lose all effectiveness.

I should have known to resist those mental attacks, but instead I was troubled by them.

RECOGNIZING THE SPIRIT OF PRAYER

Since I didn't recognize this sense of oppression and depression as the spirit of prayer, I would endeavor to resist it; yet, as I resisted, there would only be an increase of these things.

The Holy Spirit was endeavoring to get me to cooperate with Him in this spirit of prayer. I should have given myself to speaking in other tongues, for then I would have been cooperating with the Holy Spirit in prayer. I should have prayed in other tongues until I sensed the oppression and depression lift.

E.W. Kenyon describes this same prayer burden in his book, *In His Presence*. He writes, "The Holy Spirit in us oft-times makes intercession that cannot be uttered in words.

"Oft-times we are depressed; we cannot understand it or see any reason for it; it is the Holy Spirit in agony reaching through us to the Father.

"If our spirits were only fruitful (sensitive to the Holy Spirit), perhaps we could understand the language and agony of the Spirit in His mighty outreaching toward the throne of grace."

When the spirit of prayer moves on a believer like this, as we give ourselves to praying in other tongues, whenever the thing we are praying for is accomplished, the spirit of prayer will lift. When it lifts you might sing in tongues, you might start laughing, or just seem light, sensing the lifting of that burden. This is what the old-timers called "praying through."

Because I was a spiritual baby and didn't understand these things, I didn't take the time to cooperate with the Spirit through speaking in other tongues as I should have, so the prayer burden didn't lift, it would stay on me for days; but I was only troubled by it.

If I had known to cooperate with the Holy Spirit in these matters, God would have been able to accomplish His plan through me.

If my spirit had been more sensitive, I would have recognized this as a spiritual leading instead of thinking that I was under attack.

How important it is for us to receive instruction in these matters so that we'll know how to cooperate with the Holy Spirit, and bear much fruit in prayer.

WE MUST BE TAUGHT

In the life of Samuel, we see him as a child serving in the temple.

One night, as he lay down to go to sleep, he heard a voice call his name. He thought that Eli, the prophet who lived in the temple, was calling him, so he ran to him. Eli denied calling him and sent him back to his room to lie down.

This happened to Samuel three times, and each time, Samuel ran to Eli. On the third time, Eli perceived that it was the Lord who was calling Samuel. (It took Eli a couple of times to recognize that the Lord was visiting Samuel.)

Samuel responded to the voice all along, but he responded wrong. He didn't recognize that the Lord was calling him, so he ran to Eli instead of answering the Lord when He called.

If you don't recognize the dealings of God in your life, you won't respond right to them.

What was Samuel's help in this situation? It was Eli's instruction to him.

The third time that Samuel ran to the prophet, Eli instructed him how to respond properly to the voice he was hearing.

> *Therefore Eli said unto Samuel, Go, lie down: and*
> *it shall be, if he call thee, that THOU SHALT SAY,*
> *Speak, Lord; for thy servant heareth.*
>
> (1 Samuel 3:9)

As Samuel did as he was instructed by Eli, the Lord continued to speak to Samuel and gave him the message He came to bring.

We need to notice in this incident in Samuel's life, that although the Lord called Samuel's name, until Samuel recognized that as the Lord's Voice, and until he responded right to that voice, the Lord didn't continue speaking to him to deliver the message He came to bring.

What if Samuel had stayed in bed after hearing that voice call him, wondering who it was that was calling him? If he had never responded at all by going to Eli, he wouldn't have received instruction on how to properly respond to God.

THE EXPERIENCES OF OTHERS

As the Spirit of God began teaching me about the spirit of prayer, I began to take special note of what other ministers said in their writings in connection with prayer.

Kenyon notes in his writings that for years he would wake up feeling depressed, and didn't understand at the time that it was the spirit of prayer upon him; it was the agony of the Holy Spirit within him lifting up the burden of someone else to God.

He also noted in one of his books about feelings of depression that would sometimes be on him when he awoke in the mornings; this happened for some time before he later recognized it to be the spirit of prayer.

I also noted that those feelings of depression would sometimes be on me when I would awake in the mornings.

Many times the spirit of prayer may move on you as you awake in the morning, or right as you are drifting off to sleep because that's when the mind will be least active, and the stirrings of the Spirit are more easily perceived, and His leadings are more easily discerned.

Charles G. Finney, who was a mighty revivalist and a man of prayer who lived in the 1800's, often referred in his autobiography to the many times when his mind would become greatly troubled. After giving himself to prayer, his mind would again grow peaceful and calm. It was then that he knew that the answer to his prayer was secured.

I have learned that when my mind seems troubled and unsettled, it's because my spirit is troubled and unsettled. As I take time to pray in other tongues at those times, that troubling leaves me and a perfect peace returns to my spirit and my mind.

I've had that troubling in my spirit to last for days; but I would continue to lift the need up to God by praying in other tongues until it lifted, be it a long or a short length of time.

GOING ASIDE TO PRAY

When under a heavier spirit of prayer, I would have to stop what I was doing to go aside to lift the burden of my heart to the Lord. If that burden stayed for hours, or even days, and I had other daily responsibilities, I would go aside as often as possible to lift up the burden on my spirit to the Lord. But when the heavier spirit of prayer would move on me, I would set aside as many of the daily responsibilities as possible so that I could give myself to prayer.

Then at other times, if the spirit of prayer isn't as heavy upon me, then I'm usually able to pray as I go about my daily business, lifting my heart to the Lord all the while and praying in other tongues throughout the day; I've still been able to pray until I sense the lifting of that burden.

MISSED LEADINGS

One minister tells of an incident when they had a leading to pray for a loved one. About five minutes after they began praying, the phone rang and the minister was asked to run an errand; so, they left the house and forgot about the leading they had to pray.

A couple of hours later, they received another phone call that informed them that a loved one had been killed in an automobile accident that morning; it was the same loved one they had a leading to pray for.

If we're too busy with natural things, we can miss the leading of the Spirit, and it can cost us much.

There have been some times when I've missed the leadings given by the Spirit of God.

I had a relative I hadn't seen for decades, yet as I was getting dressed one morning, their name came up to me.

I didn't recognize it as the Spirit's leading to pray, so I just reminisced about them and the times we had played together as children, but I failed to pray for them.

About a week later, a family member called to tell me that this relative had died. They were only in their mid-forties, and left behind a spouse and two children.

It was the same relative that the Spirit had endeavored to get me to pray for, but I had missed the leading given by the Spirit.

What was the cue the Spirit gave? My relative's name came up in my spirit.

I didn't have a sense of urgency; I didn't sense that their life was in danger. Nevertheless, if I had prayed, I'm convinced their situation could have been changed.

We will miss the cues the Holy Spirit gives us if we don't give ourselves enough time in the Spirit. We must spend time speaking in other tongues so that we will keep our spirits sensitive to the leading of the Spirit. There's much to be lost if we don't stay keen in the spirit.

However, if we do miss it, we just have to repent and go on.

A WATCHMAN

About three weeks after this relative of mine died, I was leading daily prayer at our church.

After spending some time praying in other tongues, I got caught up in the Spirit, and God spoke to me saying, "I am holding you responsible to be a watchman over your family.

"The life of your relative could have been spared if you would have cooperated with My Spirit and prayed. Their situation could have been changed.

"You can't change every situation for your relatives, but some situations can be changed. If they can be changed, I *expect* them to be changed!"

There would be some things I would be unable to change. That means that it would be a change that they would have to make on their end; I couldn't make the change for them.

But there would be some situations that my faith could aid in changing, and the things that could be changed, He *expected* them to be changed! He expects me to bring my faith to their situation and do my part to lay hold of help in their behalf.

Since God has deposited and imparted so much of His Word into us, He expects us to use that to bring blessing and help to others.

What did God mean by saying He was making me accountable to be a "watchman" over my family?

Isaiah 62:6 & 7, (The Amplified Bible) reads,

I have set watchmen upon your walls, O Jerusalem, who will never hold their peace day or night; you who [are His servants and BY YOUR PRAYERS] PUT THE LORD IN REMEMBRANCE [OF HIS PROMISES], keep not silence, And give Him no rest until He establishes Jerusalem and makes her a praise in the earth.

The "watchmen" who are spoken of in this passage are

not watching for the enemy; they are putting God in remembrance of what He promised in His Word, they are watching to make sure His Word to them is fulfilled. They continue to hold God's Word up to Him until they see God's Word fulfilled in their lives, their families, their homes, and their situations.

How long were the watchmen to remind God? They were to remind Him until He established them and made them a place of praise in the earth.

You are to hold God's Word up to Him, reminding Him of His promises until that which you love and care about, that which you are praying about, becomes a place where God's will is being accomplished.

HEART SYMPTOMS

One minister told me of an experience he had when the spirit of prayer moved on him in behalf of another pastor.

As he was getting ready to preach his Sunday morning service, he began to have chest pains. He resisted the devil and claimed his healing, but the heart symptoms only continued.

Then God spoke to him and said, "I want you to go to Pastor W's church and pray for his healing."

Since he was dealing with symptoms in his own body, the minister decided he would wait until after his own morning service before going to pray for the other pastor.

After his own service had ended, the minister received a phone call informing him that Pastor W had fallen dead in the pulpit of a heart attack.

The minister realized that all the heart symptoms he had been feeling had stopped. He realized that all along he had been sensing the symptoms of the dying pastor. But because they felt so real to him, he thought that he was having problems with his own body. He had missed God by not going to pray for the other pastor before his own Sunday morning service.

God was looking for someone to cooperate with him and minister to the other pastor. Had this minister followed God's instructions and gone to lay hands on the other minister, the man would have been healed.

TUBERCULOSIS HEALED

Smith Wigglesworth told of an experience he had when he went to pray for a minister who had been bedfast with tuberculosis.

He had gone to visit the man at his home, and saw that his health had declined to the point that he looked like a mere skeleton. Wigglesworth told the man he would return to minister to him on the following day.

As Brother Wigglesworth slept that night, he was awakened with every symptom of tuberculosis fastened upon his own body. Wigglesworth rolled out of bed and onto the floor and began praying. The symptoms seemed so real that he thought that he was being attacked with tuberculosis; however, Brother Wigglesworth did the right thing by praying until those symptoms lifted from him.

138

Wigglesworth stated that he thought Satan was trying to put tuberculosis on him. But I am convinced that through the spirit of prayer, the Spirit of God was reaching out toward the throne of grace through Brother Wigglesworth in behalf of the dying man. He was accessing God's power, making tremendous power available to him.

When Wigglesworth ministered to the man the following day, he was completely healed and raised up by the power of God as the dying man responded to the power that was made available to him.

Many times the Spirit of God is searching for someone to cooperate with Him in this mighty work of prayer. The Spirit is looking for someone to make requests and release faith on the behalf of another. The Spirit helps us in this great prayer work by giving us utterance in other tongues, but we must yield and cooperate with Him.

We must be sensitive in our own spirits toward the Holy Spirit so that we will recognize His movements and stirrings within us.

Many times, those being moved upon by Him with the spirit of prayer think it's "just them," when it is the Holy Spirit seeking to employ them in a holy undertaking of prayer on the behalf of someone else who is in need.

PRAYER FOR THE LOST

In church services, when the invitation is given to be born again, a believer present in the service may sometimes feel as though they are lost and in need of salvation. They may even go so far as to answer the altar call themselves, thinking that they aren't right with God. But it's the spirit of prayer that is moving on them.

That feeling of being separated from God is them sensing the spiritual condition of someone in the service who is lost. When the Spirit of God moves on you to pray for someone who's lost, you may feel as though you yourself are lost, but you are sensing *their* great need.

Because believers don't always recognize these things, or are not as sensitive as they should be, they respond wrong by either ignoring it, or answering the altar call themselves.

What they should do is remain in their seat and pray quietly in other tongues until that sense of being lost lifts from them. If the spirit of prayer is too heavy to pray quietly, then they can quietly leave and go to a place alone to pray until that spirit of prayer lifts from them.

By cooperating with the Spirit in this way, you are making God's power available to them, which makes it easier for that lost one to make the right decision to receive Christ.

Don't misunderstand me. Your prayers don't save anyone. Jesus is the Savior.

You don't have to pray and ask God to save people; He has already sent Jesus and paid the price for their salvation. The lost must simply *receive* Jesus as their Savior.

But when you pray for the lost, you are making God's power available to them. You are causing God's power to move mightily upon them, which makes it easier for that lost one to make the right choice to receive Jesus as their

Savior; for under the influence of His mighty power, they will recognize their lost condition.

When the power of God is moving upon someone, that power brings a holy influence that stirs them toward the right decision, but still they must be the one to make the choice to receive Jesus as Savior.

When one pastor heard me teach this, he said, "Now I know how to instruct a particular member in my church. Every time I've given an altar call over the past 15 years, this man has answered it by coming forward. Now I know why."

Evidently the spirit of prayer would move on him so strong that he felt that he was lost and separated from God, when he was really sensing the condition of someone in that service who was lost.

If you don't know any better, you will think "it's just you," when it's really the spirit of prayer moving on you.

SENSING DEATH

On one occasion, we were on an overseas trip to conduct a week-long meeting.

The first evening we were in this other country, I kept sensing death; so I took time aside and began praying in other tongues. That sense of death was so real, and I realized that someone was near death.

As long as I could sense death, I continued to pray in other tongues. I didn't try to handle it mentally, trying to figure out what it was about. Instead, I just quieted my mind, and focused on my spirit. (If someone handles it mentally, they may think that death is trying to come on them.)

That sense of death lasted for a couple of hours, and then it completely lifted from me. When it lifted, a great sense of peace returned to me.

The next morning, when the pastor picked us up to drive us to the service, he told us of a friend of ours who had died the night before.

I immediately knew that was the situation I had sensed.

As we make our own spirits sensitive to the Holy Spirit, we may sense things that don't pertain to us; rather, we are sensing someone else's situation.

A SPIRITUAL DREAM

On another occasion, I had a dream about a woman I knew.

Let me take a side road and say something here about spiritual dreams.

Spiritual dreams are not likely to occur on a daily basis. Sometimes, people try to spiritualize every dream they have, but that only serves to make them spiritually unsound.

If God gives you a dream, you'll sense the power of God upon you when you awake, and you'll know the meaning of the dream when you awake. If you have to search out a meaning and try to put your own interpretation on a dream, the dream isn't from God, and needs to be forgotten.

If a dream makes you fearful, God didn't give it; it needs to be forgotten. Even if God did give you a dream that revealed danger to you, it wouldn't make you fearful.

Any dream that makes you fearful, or any dream that you don't know the meaning of when you awaken, is to be rejected, forgotten, and not touched again in your thought life.

We don't seek for spiritual dreams because we have no scriptural basis to stand upon to seek for dreams; but if God does give us one, then we should know its meaning and it will bring blessing and soundness to us.

In the dream I had about this woman, I saw her face before me. Although she was born again, she was not walking in the light of the Word.

As soon as I awoke, God spoke to me, telling me to pray for her. I began praying for her with other tongues. The longer I prayed the more distant I felt from God; I was sensing her spiritual condition.

For several hours I continued in prayer for her. There was a great heaviness and grieving upon me.

After a few hours, it lifted from me, and the grieving and heaviness was gone. Peace and lightness returned to me.

That night, we received a phone call from this woman, and she was stating how she had been neglectful toward her call from God and wanted to obey God in His plan for her life.

I rejoiced to see her recognize the dealings of God with her.

A SENSE OF LOSS

On one Saturday night, I had gone out to dinner with some friends. On the way home from the restaurant, I had a peculiar experience I had never had before. I suddenly felt as though I had lost all my own family members – spouse and children. I sensed the great grieving and loss move over me as if I had lost everything dear to me. This baffled me for a moment, for the sense of loss was so overwhelming.

When I got home, I immediately went aside and prayed in other tongues. While I was praying, God spoke to me, saying, "There's a person who will be in your Sunday morning service tomorrow who has just lost everything through divorce – their spouse, their children, their possessions."

Their overwhelming loss and grieving was so strong upon me that I wept and agonized as though it were my own loss.

After a time of praying in the Spirit for them, the burden lifted and peace returned. God then gave me a message to preach just for them that would bring them comfort and encouragement.

The Amplified Bible in James 5:16 states, *"The earnest* (heartfelt, continued) *prayer of a righteous man makes tremendous power available."*

Notice the words used: earnest, heartfelt, continued.

These words don't depict human, natural feelings or emotions that you manufacture yourself so that you'll be effective in prayer; rather, when you cooperate with the Spirit of God in prayer, you will sense how He is earnest, heartfelt and continued toward the situation He is leading you to pray about.

MORE EXPERIENCES IN PRAYER

Many times, for no apparent reason, I will feel like weeping; but I have learned that it is the Holy Spirit within me reaching out to the Father on behalf of another. I will feel just as Jesus feels for them. I am entering into a divine compassion on the behalf of someone else.

As I cooperate with the Spirit, and weep under that spirit of prayer, before long, the weeping turns to joy; the burden lifts, and lightness and peace return.

As we know Jesus' great love for humanity, we will move into a place of prayer that is flowing out of the realm of love.

There have been occasions when I have been so grieved in my spirit that it seems to affect my body. At those times, my appetite wanes, I have a great grieving in my spirit, there seems to be a knot in my stomach, I'm absorbed in prayer, and I can't fully focus on other natural duties.

Sometimes, that kind of burden has stayed on me for days, but as I continue to pray in other tongues, it will lift after a period of time. (Again, if you're not acquainted with these things, you may be tempted to think that something is the matter with you, but learn to quiet the mind, focus on your spirit, and cooperate with the Holy Spirit in these matters.)

On some occasions, when the spirit of prayer moves on me, it seems as though all my strength is drained from me; but as I cooperate with the Spirit, and give myself to praying in other tongues, that prayer burden will lift, and my strength returns and I am refreshed.

After one prayer burden lifts from you, sometimes another will immediately come. The reason for that is that when you're responding to the spirit of prayer, you're available to God and He will continue to move on you in that way.

DEVELOP YOUR PRAYER LIFE

The more you give yourself to prayer, the more the Holy Spirit will be able to use you, and the more experiences you will have with the Holy Spirit in prayer. The more you cooperate with the Spirit in prayer, the more sensitive you'll be to the Spirit and you'll be quick to recognize His dealings and movements.

For the Holy Spirit to use you in prayer, you must make yourself available to Him. If you are available to Him, you'll respond to Him when He moves within you or upon you.

However, you don't have to wait for Him to move on you to pray. You can set yourself to pray any time you choose. In fact, the more you set yourself to pray, the more He will move on you with the spirit of prayer.

You must keep yourself stirred in the direction of prayer if you are going to be effective in prayer. Feed on sound teachings on prayer; it will keep your prayer life stirred. Make time to spend in prayer every day, and participate in prayer meetings in your local church.

When the Holy Spirit needs to give a prayer assignment to someone, He's going to use someone who prays. He won't be able to use someone who hasn't taken time to develop their prayer life.

It's your job to develop your prayer life, not God's.

Those who were used mightily in prayer gave themselves to prayer; they just kept at it and became proficient in it.

Daniel was used mightily of God in prayer, but the Word tells us in Daniel 9:3, *"And I SET MY FACE unto the Lord God, to seek by prayer and supplications..."* That's not something God did, that's something Daniel did; he gave himself to prayer.

The apostles in the early days of the church were used mightily in prayer, but they declared in Acts 6:4, *"we will give ourselves continually to prayer."* No one is called to prayer in the same way that someone is called to stand in a fivefold office. We are all to give ourselves to prayer.

The more we give ourselves to prayer, the more God will be able to use us in this great work. Every believer is instructed to pray. It's something we must all give ourselves to. It's not something that just a few are called to; it is a privilege with which we all must be responsible.

RECOMMENDED READING ON PRAYER

Kenneth E. Hagin
  Prayer Bible Study Course
  The Art of Prayer

Phil & Fern Halverson
  Unseen Forces Beyond This World

Smith Wigglesworth
  Ever Increasing Faith

E.W. Kenyon
  In His Presence

Charles Finney
  The Autobiography of Charles Finney

BOOKS BY DR. ED DUFRESNE

Praying God's Word

Devil, Don't Touch My Stuff

There's a Healer In The House

Faithfulness: The Road to Divine Promotion

The Footsteps Of A Prophet

Golden Nuggets For Longevity

BOOKS BY NANCY DUFRESNE

Daily Healing Bread From God's Table

His Presence Shall Be My Dwelling Place

Victory In The Name

*There Came A Sound From Heaven:
The Life Story of Ed Dufresne*

The Healer Divine

Visitations From God

Responding To The Holy Spirit

God: The Revealer of Secrets

A Supernatural Prayer Life

For a complete list of ministry materials, write to:

Ed Dufresne Ministries
P.O. Box 1010, Murrieta, CA 92564
or call (951) 696-9258,
or visit our web site at www.eddufresne.org